The House on Sylvia Street

30 years, 300 medically fragile foster

children, and a whole lot of sock monkeys

To Meredith

Judy Bordeaux

JUDY BORDEAUX

CLOUD RIDGE PRESS

ISBN: 1496079418
ISBN-13: 9781496079411
Library of Congress Control Number: 2014903929
CreateSpace Independent Publishing Platform
North Charleston, South Carolina

Dedicated to my granddaughters,
Lily,
Bly,
and Sawyer

ACKNOWLEDGEMENTS

I WOULD BE remiss if I didn't first thank my mentor Dori Yang Jones. I am equally grateful for Julie Woodward's support and good eye. Meredith Bailey's editing has been crucial, and I so appreciate Kathy Campbell's patience and receptivity in creating a cover design. Others whose help was invaluable along the way include Cheri Stefani, Diana Roger, Mary Seaton, Alex Rea, Parul Houlilhan, Sally Gray, James Reddick, Nailla Vanderkolk, Lisa Baty, Roosevelt Travis, Dawn Grace Peters, and Ann Huber.

CONTENTS

Instructions for Living a Life
Pay attention.
Be astonished.
Tell about it.

Mary Oliver

SPRING

SYLVIA STREET

Don't try to find Sylvia Street in a West Coast city using Google maps. It isn't there. What I have written about the events and people in Beth's house is true, but she doesn't live on Sylvia Street and her name isn't Beth. As she herself put it, "The names and places have been changed to protect the innocent and confuse the guilty."

Beth is a former classmate with whom I reconnected through reunions. In an email title "Take a Deep Breath," I told I wanted to come shadow her for a few days in order to write about her life as a foster mom for medically fragile kids. She suggested that the second week in March might be interesting because two children were transitioning to adoption and one girl had a variety of medical appointments to attend.

I was the one who should have taken a deep breath. I plunged into Beth's life at quarter after eight on a Tuesday morning and came up for air Thursday night at nine. That week, not including me who went to a hotel each night, seven people lived in the house on Sylvia Street, ranging from tiny sixteen-month-old Jeffrey, just learning to walk and struggling with food issues, to twenty-eight-year-old David, legally blind and challenged by cerebral palsy and developmental difficulties. Other children filled in the life stages in between: Head Start, first grade, middle school, high school, and post high school.

This first visit, which turned out to be just one of several I made over the next twelve months, intrigued me, but I had no idea of what a glorious and achingly beautiful household they would become for me.

TUESDAY

WHEN I ARRIVE on the quiet and well-tended street, Beth's house stands out because it has a gate at the top of the porch steps and a flag with a dapper Irish Snoopy in a green hat hanging from a rafter. The house is in an old neighborhood, with a mixed population. Across the street an elderly woman lives in the home where she spent her childhood. Down the block is a family with three generations under one roof. Some households are young professionals who have remodeled but kept the classic early twentieth-century look. An artist and her children also live across the street.

I notice two vans in Beth's driveway: one that seats fifteen and one that seats eight. As I step onto the large covered porch that extends the width of the house, I notice a small trampoline, a porch swing, a wagon, a toy lawn mower, and several riding toys.

Breakfast is mostly over when I arrive. Beth is drinking a Diet Pepsi: "My dirty little secret." she laughs. Considering how many people have to get out the door in the next hour, it's amazingly calm in the large clean living room with braided rugs. A dining table with eight chairs sits at one end, and a pass-through window shows a spacious kitchen. Beth has just put a load of laundry in the washer and given Jeffrey a bottle. She signs to twenty-four-year-old Coleen, who is severely hearing impaired and curled up in an easy chair texting and watching television, that she needs to bathe and change Jeffrey, who has just thrown up much of his milk. He must be ready when the caseworker picks him up for his supervised visit with parents.

Beth helps four-year-old Jaytee, too busy zooming around to concentrate on getting ready to leave, finish dressing. She says goodbye to Markie, who's off to post-high school life-skills classes. Markie's excited because today they're visiting the animal shelter. Markie gives Daisy, her fluffy white dog, a farewell snuggle and is cheerfully out the door. Shontel, when reminded, takes care of getting the goldfish crackers from the cupboard into a backpack. It's her day to bring the class snack to her first grade classroom. Beth tapes a water guard over fourteen-year-old Mercedes's chest dialysis catheter port so she can shower and sends her into the bathroom with a reminder to be ready to leave for a morning of medical appointments as soon as she returns from dropping off the little ones.

While waiting for everyone else to get ready, Shontel tells me that she's not going to check out any more library books because Monday is her last day at school. Both she and her brother are moving, because they are about to be adopted.

"I'm going to a new school." Shontel tells me. "It might be hard."

I nod in agreement, but offer a suggestion: "Maybe the new school will have a library with books you've never seen."

"Maybe....." she replies, but her grimace tells me she is not convinced that fresh library books will make the move any easier.

So now I've met everyone living in the house except David, whom I will meet this afternoon. Let me tell you a little more about each child. We'll start with Baby Jeffrey. He's sixteen months old, but you'd never guess that. He's tiny, delightfully elfin, and, unfortunately delayed. Born prematurely, along with a twin brother who didn't survive, he was unable to eat, and had to be fed by a tube for quite a while. Even now, nutrition is a challenge. Despite extensive work finding the right formula, it's difficult for him to keep a bottle down. Tiny finger-food puffs that dissolve in the mouth are the only solid food he can handle. Though he's just starting to walk, and doesn't yet make the variety of sounds you would expect from a sixteen-month-old, he has a killer smile.

Next to Beth, Jeffrey is most comfortable with Coleen, the tallest person in the house, because during the day she often cares for him. She too was a premature twin like Jeffrey, but she was also born almost completely deaf. A cochlear implant has given Coleen *some* hearing in one ear, but she is nonetheless challenged by significant hearing loss. While she was still an infant she was adopted by Beth, and now as an adult who receives supplemental security income (SSO), she lives at home and works part time as her mother's helper.

Jaytee couldn't be a more handsome little four-year-old boy with black curls, dark eyes, and coffee-colored skin. He is, however, a handful, as I was to discover over the next few days. That morning, it did surprise me that he couldn't dress himself, but otherwise I was clueless to the challenges he offers to Beth and his Head Start teachers.

Jaytee's sister, Shontel, is a bright first grader who has lived with Beth since she was two, when Jaytee was born and came to the Sylvia Street house. She's wiry, with a glorious mane of black hair, a vivid imagination, and an independent streak. Medication for her hyperactivity has enabled her to focus and learn, transforming her into a self-sufficient six year-old.

Markie is the noisy one in the house, and when there's nobody around to listen to her, she talks to Daisy, her dog. Markie has just turned twenty, but her delays and disabilities make her seem much younger. While she was not diagnosed as an infant with fetal alcohol syndrome – the diagnosis requires very specific documentation that wasn't gathered – she exhibits the traits that are typical of that syndrome, For example, the random thoughts or reactions that someone else might just *think,* Markie verbalizes.

"That color doesn't look so good on you." she had said to Beth this morning, totally unaware of the impact of her words.

— 7 —

Her round face usually radiates either optimism or anger, with little in between. She has spent most of her life at Beth's house, and although she recently reconnected with her birth father, Beth and the other children are the only family she has ever known.

As noisy as Markie is, Mercedes is quiet. Fourteen and very sick, she needs Beth's nursing skills perhaps more than anyone else in the house. But given her age and disposition, she would probably be quiet if she were healthy. She can't attend school because of her health, but she often has a book or school-issued laptop in her hands.

And Beth? She's a sturdily built, no-jewelry, no-makeup, no-nonsense woman in her mid-sixties. Her mid-length gray hair waves in natural curls. Her gait and her occasional sighs on sitting or standing suggest to me that arthritis plagues her.

So there we have it – elfin Baby Jeffrey, energetic, curly-topped four-year old Jaytee, his bright-eyed sister, Shontel, young teen Mercedes with her soft voice, chattering twenty-year-old Markie, quiet and responsible adult Coleen with major hearing losses, Beth, the mom, and twenty-eight-year-old David, whom we will meet later.

⌒⌒

USING THE SMALLER van Beth and I take Shontel to school, and then drop Jaytee off at Head Start. Beth banters and laughs with the teacher about an NBA basketball game from the night before.

"You actually expected those guys to lose? Are you kidding?" They both love basketball.

On the way home, Beth tells me a little bit about her adopted son David, who wasn't up yet when we left. He's not an early riser, she shared with me, but he does his exercises when he first awakes. Then he does them again at one o'clock, regardless of when he got up. She tells me that when I do meet him, he will interview me, and probably ask me first about my vacuum cleaner. For his whole life, David has loved vacuum cleaners, shop vacs, dust busters – you name it. He enjoys cleaning activities of all kinds: dusting, mopping, washing and sweeping. But vacuuming is a life-long preoccupation, love, and obsession. Appropriately, David works on Monday mornings at their church, vacuuming and cleaning the pews. Women in the congregation who come to count the money collected on Sunday are so charmed by David that they have a tea and cookie break with him every week.

We arrive back at the house to get Mercedes. The caseworker has already picked up Jeffrey.

Beth reminds Coleen that there is laundry to fold, and then we're off to the hospital. Mercedes looks stylish: swishy little black skirt over leggings, tennis shoes with bright aqua laces, and a small purple handbag slung over her shoulder. Only the puffiness in her face from steroid medication would suggest an ill child.

"You might wipe off a little of that blue eye shadow," Beth comments with smiling eyes, "so they don't think I've hit you!"

Mercedes rolls her eyes, and then takes a tissue out of her handbag and dabs her eyelids.

The hospital grounds are beautiful, and large floor-to-sky windows offer beautiful views of trees, sky, and city skyline. This is especially important for sick children who spend too much time confined in a hospital, I think, but Mercedes seems unaffected: *same old hospital, maybe,* I surmise. In the walkways and waiting area, splashes of color in the flooring, on walls, and in large sculptures or mobiles add whimsy without making the place feel like a theme park. The place is bustling with activity, but not crowded. I notice that Mercedes holds Beth's arm when we are walking to the reception area. Occasionally her left side gives out for thirty seconds or so. It is an unexplained side effect of either her lupus or the *cryptococcus meningitis,* an infection of the lining of the brain that hospitalized her for most of the winter. Several people, even the parking attendant outside, greet Beth by name, and Mercedes receives hugs, smiles and comments about how good she looks.

"Mercedes, seeing you just made my day!" says a beaming doctor passing through the reception area.

In the waiting room, Mercedes listens to her iPod and Beth pulls out her book. She laughs aloud as she reads. Her easy-going nature is coupled with a well-developed sense of humor that keeps a twinkle in her eye most of the time.

When the nurse calls for Mercedes, we start for the exam room, but the girl's left leg gives out part way down the hall. For almost a minute, everyone just waits. No alarm, no panic, no calling attention to this pause. They protect this young teen's dignity. Mercedes recovers, and we proceed into the exam room. A bit of wheezing related to her current cough concerns the doctor, who has cared for her through her bouts with meningitis and several rounds of pneumonia.

"We'll keep a close eye on that," the doctor says. "We might need a chest x-ray this week."

"Well, we're here at the hospital every day for the next several days," Beth says, "so if the need comes up, we'll already be here."

The doctor's expression and slight nod of her head tells me that she trusts Beth's expertise and experience. When the kidney specialist comes in for the next appointment, Mercedes makes it clear that she likes this doctor and perks up. This doctor talks more to the girl and less to Beth. Mercedes responds to the doctor's questions in full sentences, and asks several of her own,

"What is my blood type?" She is thrilled to hear that it's B positive, the same type as an adult half-brother. "Can he give me a kidney? How soon can I get a kidney?" Unspoken: Dialysis three times a week is tough.

The doctor struggles to keep a neutral expression on her face. "Honey, we need to get you stronger before we can even think about that." The unstated fact is that having lupus, an autoimmune disease, means that her immune system might not only reject the new kidney but possibly flare up and attack some of her other organs.

The next doctor to enter is the heart specialist. Mercedes is tired by this time and lies on the exam table for the visit, even though the only physical exam procedure is listening to her heart. The doctor reports that some of the damage from her lupus, or perhaps a side effect from one of her medications, seems to be healing. Next, we go upstairs for an echocardiogram. In the waiting room, Beth reminds Mercedes how the procedure will work. She'll have to take off her metal necklace and change into a gown. They will smear a gel on her chest when they start.

When we leave the hospital, Beth asks Mercedes what she wants for lunch. She opts for Mexican food. I sense that the morning's ordeal means a special lunch, as opposed to a steady diet of dining out. If I'd just experienced the medical morning that she had, I'd want someone to take me out for the kind of food I like.

Looking at the menu, Beth asks in a silly voice, "So, okay, do you want the Mexican food with little salt or the Mexican food with little salt?" It's a silly way of reminding Mercedes that her choices of food and beverage have to be limited both in calorie intact and in sodium content. The girl tentatively makes a choice and, although her head is still bent down over the menu, her eyes look to Beth for confirmation. Beth nods proudly. Mercedes is learning to self-monitor.

Beth then takes Mercedes to an electronics store because her phone is not working. This is the most important stop of the day for Mercedes. Since she can't go to school, her phone is an emotional lifeline. At this point she doesn't see relatives or old school friends, and texting or talking on the phone fills part of the hole in life.

After I return from checking into my hotel, I notice two young girls having a tea party in their yard across the street from Beth's house. They have hung ribbons and brightly colored umbrellas in the small tree above their tea table. Markie returns from her day at the animal shelter and, regardless of the differences in age, joins them. The young ones are on little chairs; Markie is sitting cross legged on the lawn. All three are drinking pretend tea.

Then I spot an attractive young woman, with her red pony-tail bobbing, coming down the street jauntily pushing a stroller. A young child walks at her side. Wait a minute! That's Shontel, I realize. Coleen and Baby Jeffrey, back home from supervised visits with his parents, have picked Shontel up from school. They stop to chat under the festooned tree, and Shontel joins the tea party. Maybe it's the early spring sunshine on the ribbons, or the easy way the little hostesses welcome the new tea drinkers: I am touched by the scene.

As I watch the tea party revelers from my car window, Beth and Mercedes arrive home. David, who is wearing bright orange safety vest and has been out riding in the neighborhood on his large adult trike, also pulls into the driveway, and everyone chats amicably for a few minutes. Mercedes goes inside to nap. Beth starts another load of laundry and signs with Coleen, who will need to care for Jeffrey for an hour while Beth and I take Shontel to a counseling appointment.

We drive with Shontel to a counseling center specializing in foster children and adoptees. This is one of several play therapy sessions for Shontel in preparation for her upcoming adoption.

On the way Shontel asks, "Mommy, why do I like to follow you around?"

Beth softly throws the question back to her, "Why *do* you like to follow me around?"

With a little nudging, Shontel is able to say, "I like being with you." She's grieving, Beth later explains, because she's leaving for a new home in less than a week, and this is the processing of that grief.

At the center Shontel is given a bag of snacks and meets with a counselor. A woman comes in a few minutes later and asks if Beth has a change of pants. Shontel has had an accident. Not common for Shontel, but common for kids in a major life-changing transition, I learn. While we are waiting, another young girl checks in for her counseling sessions. She and Beth greet each other warmly. "Mama Beth!" the girl exclaims. They talk a bit about fourth grade, and the drama class she has joined. Her name is Roxie and she had lived with Beth for several years before she was adopted. I recognize her face from one of the many framed school photos on a high shelf in Beth's house.

Appointment over, we pick up Jaytee from Head Start. He suddenly stops walking to the car when something on the sidewalk catches his attention. Despite the late hour, Beth doesn't urge him to move along. She waits and bends down to share his momentary fascination. She notices that Jaytee has completely torn out the back of his pants. He cannot explain how that happened. When we get home, Beth gives Jeffrey a bottle and snuggles with him while she hears about Markie's day and answers David's random questions.

I finally get to meet David. He's slender and earnest, impeccably dressed, and walks with a slight limp. After Beth introduces us, he comes and sits next to me on the couch. "So," he begins enthusiastically, "what kind of vacuum cleaner do you use? I hope it doesn't have a bag. Bagless is much better, unless it's a cheap vacuum. Is it plastic or metal? How long is the cord? A long cord is really important so you don't have to keep changing it to a new outlet. Do you remember where you bought it? How often do you vacuum out your car? You use the big vacuums at gas stations? Oh, they just eat quarters!" His rapid-fire delivery leaves little time for answers.

Eventually our conversation moves to other topics, like where I live? Do I have a dog? David doesn't want to talk about himself. He is really interested in my life – well in certain aspects of my life. I am smitten. I understand why the Monday morning money ladies at the church share cookies with him. "Do you believe in God?" he abruptly asks me. He goes to the CD player on the fireplace mantel and with much effort finds and plays "In the Garden."

"Have you heard of this?" he asks.

Markie rolls her eyes. "Not that music again!"

"Oh, I know this song. Our choir is singing it in two weeks." David does a full body wiggle and claps his hands; he is thrilled that I know it.

"Where are you singing it?"

"It's for a memorial service." I casually offer. That's a mistake on my part, because now he's suddenly very concerned about the person who died. I assure him that she led a rich life before she passed, and then we hum along with the music. Although it is his favorite song, he doesn't know the words.

Beth announces to everyone that it will be pizza night (from the freezer) because she has line dancing class. I think to myself: *You're leaving this crew and going dancing?*" But Jeffrey, Jaytee and Shontel will be in bed soon, and Coleen is willing and comfortable handling the last few minutes of their day. David, Markie, and Mercedes know their household responsibilities regarding dinner and cleanup, and seem equally comfortable settling into the evening.

Soon Beth and I are off to a local community center. She has a permit for a disabled parking space right in front of the center, but tonight the van carries two healthy adults, so we don't use it. Inside we join ten middle-aged and elderly women in an hour of line-dancing instruction. Two wear cowgirl boots. Others are in tennis shoes. Some wear jeans, some sweats, and some polyester slacks. They spread out in the room, facing one of the wall-to-ceiling mirrors. The teacher, a perfectly-coifed woman in a stylish Western shirt and skirt who looks much younger than her seventy-some years, reviews the steps of the first dance and then starts the CD player. With total concentration the class members dance their way through the song. They go through the same routine with each dance. I attempt to join in on some of the dances.

Beth says she dances for her health, and it helps with her arthritis. I see that it's also a break from the stresses of the day and the night ahead. When you're line dancing, you're in the moment. Moving though the steps takes concentration, and if your mind wanders to some other part of your life, you fall out of the rhythm of the dance.

Sweaty and feeling good after class, Beth and I drive back to Sylvia Street. We're quiet in the car. Questions about kids and medical conditions can wait.

After saying our goodbyes, I head back to my motel to type up my impressions of the day. Beth will hopefully sit down for a while with her book, but I know that she has to hook up Mercedes's overnight nutrition pump and read and then respond in a back- and-forth journal that accompanies Baby Jeffrey to his twice weekly parental visits. She writes a message about him to the biological parents prior to each visit, and then they each write back to her after their individual visits with their son. They visit separately because a restraining order keeps them from seeing each other. Beth will also need to check her email and arrange for the next visit of the tutor provided by the school district for Mercedes. Before she turns in, she'll set the alarm for quarter past five, because Wednesday is dialysis day, and she'll need to have Mercedes at the hospital by six.

All I need to do? Turn off my computer, brush my teeth, check the door, and turn off the light.

THE LAUNDRY ROOM

THERE'S A CHILDHOOD rhyme about days of the week that begins, "Today is wash day, today is wash day. Monday wash day..." Some people have a particular wash day. My brother-in-law likes the routine of washing sheets and towels on Thursday and clothes on Friday. A cousin starts a load of wash before she heads for bed once a week. Some people do laundry on the weekend when they have more time. Others wait until they have enough to justify a trip to the Laundromat. But not Beth

Every day is wash day for Beth. She waits until Shontel is awake to start a load, since the girl's room abuts the laundry room. In the early mornings before the children are up, Beth takes care of paperwork, sorts medications, washes Mercedes's nutrition pump, and maybe has a Diet Pepsi in peace. But once the household is awake it's time for the first wash load of the day! Throughout the day, more loads are started.

The laundry room, right off the kitchen, is large and bright with windows on one wall. Several years ago, when Beth remodeled the house, she was intentional about creating an efficient space for doing the laundry for an eight-or-nine-person household. Jaytee and Jeffrey seem to accumulate the largest amount of dirty clothes. Jaytee often goes through more than one outfit a day because he has enjoyed a mud puddle or had an accident in his pants. Jeffrey frequently throws up on himself, on burp cloths, blankets, and maybe the clothes of whoever is holding him. Children with medical issues may need a change of bedding more often than others, but at a minimum, there are sixteen sheets a week that need washing. Five tall wire laundry hampers line one wall and hold dirty laundry, sorted by type: bath towels, sheets; jeans. Above the hampers a long shelf holds clean and folded towels and bedding. A giant container of laundry detergent marked "100 loads" sits on the dryer. It will last about a month. A counter spanning the length of the long wall is stacked with piles of sorted and folded clean laundry waiting to be delivered to the bedrooms or bathrooms. On the floor sit several full laundry baskets of items just out of the dryer waiting to be sorted. I try to make sense of the five hampers and piles of clean laundry. It might include 56 pairs of socks per week. A comic taped to the wall shows a mountain of socks and a woman holding a lit match to the pile. The caption reads, "Matching the socks."

Handling the clean laundry is Coleen's task. She's free of any mealtime or kitchen duty, but sorting, folding, and delivering the household's clean laundry is an everyday job. Several times during the week I find Coleen sitting cross legged on the floor, which is always clean thanks to David, surrounded by burp cloths, kid's pajamas, socks, clothes and towels. She seems content. She listens to her iPod with the ear-bud in her one ear with some hearing and the volume cranked up very loud. If laundry management here is not exactly clockwork, it is for sure an efficient system.

Beth's Bedroom

While the other upstairs rooms in the house are intentionally clutter free, Beth's room is full of stuff. In one corner sit cartons of snack foods and drinks that she saves from the kitchen so that she can pull them out for specific kids at specific times. Lots and lots of handmade gifts and knickknacks from numerous children, many unwanted, but too precious for her to toss she admits, line the shelves, the bureau, and the floor. There are dozens of photo albums and thousands of loose photos in boxes, some sorted and some not.

One of her photos is of the royal court for the junior-senior prom in 1954 in the small town where Beth and I grew up. In first grade, she and I, along with two little boys, were selected to be the flower court. A teenager on the prom committee had convinced her parents to provide the two girls in the court with pretty dresses from their clothing store. In the black-and-white photo taken that evening, Beth's blond curls frame a serious face. We all look a little scared, but sit prim and proper in front of the high school king and queen. Nobody looks poor. But prom photos, even of flower-court children, can be deceiving.

The town where we grew up served the area loggers, cattle ranchers, and apple orchardists. Ranches, orchards, sawmills? Don't get the wrong idea of a booming economy. That part of the county had just two mill owners, four cattle-ranching families, and three large orchards. More numerous were the low-pay loggers and mill workers, ranch hands, orchard workers, and fruit-packing shed workers.

The other "owners" had small orchards that would barely support a family. One or occasionally two doctors served the town. Seven small churches served the community. The town was not prosperous, and Beth's family was poorer than most.

Her father was a logger some seasons and a rodeo rider during the summer, gone from home a lot and following the small town rodeo circuit. When she was still in elementary school, her father and mother divorced, and she lived with her mother and brothers in a small rental house in a bleak part of town near the lumber mill. Her mom became the cook at one of the town's two cafes. While families and teenagers might order hamburgers at the other café and listen to top-forty music on the juke box, single men who lived at the Graystone Hotel and ate all their meals out, truckers passing through, or men wanting a drink on the way home from work might stop at the Hitching Post for chicken fried steak. The juke box played country-western music, and a punch tab display (a paper ticket gambling game) sat at one end of the long counter that ran the length of the room. Because her mom worked in the evenings, Beth had to watch her two younger brothers after school and fix dinner for the three of them.

The children who lived in the country and took the school bus home often thought the "town kids" had it so lucky because they were free to run around town. For Beth, this meant she was "free" to clean the house and do the grocery shopping. Since it was the 1950's, all of the three small grocery stores in town would be closed when her mom got off work so Beth would select what they needed. The grocer would put the items on the mom's credit account and deliver the food to their house on his way home when the store closed. They didn't have a car; they didn't have a phone. They were poor in a poor town.

"I don't remember feeling poor." Beth says. "We always had enough to eat and clothes to wear, and, best of all, Mom paid for a children's book subscription service for me, so there were always new books arriving. Like Mercedes's memory of her early years, I realize, it was just my life, not my life of poverty. I do remember thinking that Mom was the only single parent in town." She might have been right.

Sensitivity to family issues and poverty were not strong in that decade in that rural community, and the town could have ground Beth down. For example, I remember that one of our classmates, Myrna, arrived for a week at a nearby forest camp when we were nine years old with a piece of cardboard and an army blanket. All the other campers had mattress pads, sleeping bags, and pillows for the bunk room. No leaders or parent drivers thought about Myrna's home life and lack of camp bedding ahead of time or raised an eyebrow when the other campers teased the girl. Saving Myrna from the scorn of bunk mates, including me, for her "choice" of sleeping gear was not a concept of that time or place. Some of the poorest classmates, including Myrna, missed a lot of school, performed poorly in their studies, and as a result, never earned a diploma. Teen pregnancy ended formal education for several.

Beth, on the other hand, loved reading from a young age. "I remember Mom reading to me all the time when I not yet in school. I think her attention and nurturing provided me a solid foundation. And I loved school."

Looking through old high school yearbooks, I was reminded of Beth's energy and talent. She worked on the yearbook staff and belonged to honor society. She was active in the thespian club, and had the leading role in their production of The Wizard of Oz. In fact, in her senior year her classmates voted her "Most Dramatic." In one of my yearbooks, Beth wrote a silly message that presaged the spirit and advocacy that would later be evidenced in her fostering. The yearbook staff had added a bit of whimsy to the blank signing pages at the back by including a three-by-five-inch blank box with a little cartoon animal saying "Do Not Write in This Square!" Beth chose to write in that box and next to it the simple question: WHY?

In high school, Beth worked part time as a housekeeper for her high school English teacher. For many, that certified for sure that

Beth was bright. The teacher always hired a girl, and she always picked a smart but disadvantaged girl.

After graduation, Beth left the town to attend nursing school, partly on scholarships that the English teacher had helped her secure. She married Ed, who had grown up just a few doors down from her home. In the early years of their marriage she worked as a camp nurse in the Catskills, an obstetrics nurse, and a childbirth educator. Shortly after the birth of her first biological child, she started taking in foster children.

Beth knew as a child that she wanted to be a foster mom. "I always loved babies from an early age," she mused, "and I loved the books about big families, books like Cheaper by the Dozen. I didn't want to give birth to twelve children, though." Her nursing degree made her very valuable in the world of fostering: for children who need nursing care, and who need someone who can navigate the medical system for them, a caretaker like Beth is essential if their families can't or aren't willing to take on the responsibility.

When her marriage ended, Beth stayed in the house the couple had bought on Sylvia Street, and she developed a way to not only survive and raise her three biological children, but to use her nursing skills. Equally important, she also fulfilled that childhood dream of several kids around the dinner table.

Looking at the arc of Beth's life, it's clear that a bright and resourceful girl moved away from poverty, but took with her a compassion for the vulnerable. "Been there," she seems to say. Early responsibilities gave her life skills. Books gave her the larger world. She mixed her hard-scrabble life with the life she encountered in what she read. She perhaps has always had what some might call an inner compass. That compass allowed her to navigate out of an ostensibly bleak small town, into a life that at age sixty-three, means over three hundred kids have eaten at her table and been hugged and tucked into bed, perhaps with an IV, a shot, or a last dose of medication.

The Bathroom

THE UPSTAIRS BATHROOM, *while not elegantly decorated, is clean and very functional. The tub/shower combination has, naturally, a big bucket of bath toys. A utilitarian shampoo and body wash dispenser is mounted on the wall. The shelf behind the mirror contains no medications; they're all in a high and hard to reach kitchen cupboard. The counter around the sink is five or six feet long. It would provide plenty of room for twin sinks, but instead, Beth opted during her remodel to have one large oblong sink installed, big enough to easily bathe a baby or toddler, and a long counter next to it for drying and dressing a small child. This is where Baby Jeffrey has his very frequent baths; it's where many, many babies have been bathed.*

Beth often takes in babies. Because of her experience, expertise, and willingness, she is frequently called upon when the state has a baby with failure-to-thrive issues. Failure to thrive is a broad term for a baby that doesn't meet expected standards for growth. It can happen as a result of either social or biological factors: parental neglect, disease, or a medical disorder. A child who has trouble eating because of prematurity may not take in enough calories to thrive. Failure to bond to a specific caretaker can cause or exacerbate the situation.

Years ago, Ramona was one such premature baby. Her mother gave her up at birth, and because there was no identified father or relative, she became a ward of the state. When released from the hospital, she went to Beth's arms on Sylvia Street. In a perfect world, Ramona would have been available for adoption as soon as her health stabilized. As an American Indian, her situation was more complicated.

The Indian Child Welfare Act, enacted in 1978 strives to keep Native American children with Native American families. The law was enacted for good reason. From the 1880's to the 1920's, the United States government forcibly removed many children from their parents and placed them in boarding schools where every attempt was made to erase their "Indian-ness." Based on the thinking that assimilation was in the children's best interest, they were kept away from their families and traditions. Documented stories of cruelty and abuse in these military style schools abound. Even when federally run schools were closed throughout the country, many Native children were still removed from their families by a foster care system that ignored the importance of family and culture, or perhaps worked intentionally to place children away from family and culture.

Cultural memories of forced removal remain. Lawsuits filed in the last ten years brought forward by Native adults who were victims of abuse as children in mid-20th century boarding schools in the Northwest speak to ongoing issues of pain. Is it any wonder that lingering doubts exist for some about the government's wisdom or thoughtfulness in regard to American Indian children? In fact, in 2012, the Port Gamble S'Klallam tribe severed state oversight and assumed total control of guardianship, foster care, and adoption of its own children.

The Indian Child Welfare Act is an attempt to correct former wrongs. It requires Child Protective Services, as well as other agencies, to follow specific protocols when American Indian children are removed from their homes. Active efforts begin to contact the child's tribe, and placement preferences for the child apply.

All well and good, except that Ramona's mother was an urban Native American disconnected from her roots. Identifying her tribe, ascertaining the tribal enrollment rights, and determining who should care for Ramona was a cumbersome and slow-moving process. It was bureaucracy at its worst.

Meanwhile a young Native American couple in their thirties who lived in the area was willing to adopt Ramona. But since they were not of the same tribe, the baby could not be immediately placed with them. The term American Indian is broad, encompassing many tribes; one could be Navaho, Tlingit, Swinomish, or Lakota Sioux, just as a European could be French or Lithuanian.

All in all, the paperwork took much longer than expected. As Beth explains the situation, her frustration with the bureaucracy those many years ago shows in her voice. She runs her hands through her hair and then shakes her head, as if to shake off the memory of her impatience. There was, after all, a happy ending: Ramona had many, many baths in Beth's big bathroom sink, and then, thankfully, she joined a permanent family, the one who had wanted her from the beginning.

NEXT TO THE sink on the counter sits a roll of paper towels in an attractive vertical holder. At first I was surprised. In this environmentally friendly house where the dinner napkins are cloth, and recycling and composting are carefully monitored, paper towels instead of cloth hand towels seemed odd. But immunity issues and infections are important considerations in a house full of medically fragile children.

Consider Alily, who several years ago lived with Beth through her high school years. A rare autoimmune disease required her to have platelet transfusions weekly, and her damaged immune system meant that she could not attend school. Paper towels in the bathroom would be just one of many accommodations for her as well as other ill children.

While Alily lived with her, Beth was in contact with the girl's parents, part of a large extended South Pacific Islander family living *in the city. Alily became a ward of the state in order to facilitate her medical care, which was necessary because the family was not in an economic position to care for her or to deal with the complicated maze of Alily's specific medical needs. At first, Beth said, the parents were reticent and afraid, and for good reason, considering the number of young girls from their island being kidnapped or lured into prostitution. However, the parents attended most of Alily's medical appointments, where a translator was present, and eventually Beth became, in a way, another part of the extended family. For example, she was one of the very few European-American guests at the wedding and banquet for Alily's sister.*

When she first moved to Sylvia Street, Alily's English was not strong. However, living in a house full of English speakers helped her language skills dramatically. She even went on to earn a high school diploma through her homeschooling program. This is especially impressive given the grim statistics about graduation rates for foster kids in general. A successful bone marrow transplant from a family member's marrow made it possible for the girl to start producing her own platelets, and because her health improved, she was able to move back with her family shortly after she graduated from high school at age twenty.

While Ramona moved on to a new life with her new family, Alily maintains regular contact with Beth and the older children in the house, and Beth in turn, has stayed in touch with Alily's family. Two very different success stories from Sylvia Street.

WEDNESDAY

I ARRIVE AT the Sylvia Street house just after Beth has delivered Jaytee and Shontel to Head Start and elementary school. In an oddly cheerful voice, Markie reports that Jeffrey had a bad night with a fever, and then she leaves for class. Baby Jeffrey is pushing a dining chair across the room, and although his nose is running and he's coughing, and he clearly looks sick, he is grinning ear to ear. Beth is talking and laughing with him while she sits at the table filling pill boxes for Mercedes. "Is that your train, Jeffrey? Are you the engineer? Can your train blow its whistle? Toot! Toot!"

Before we leave to pick up Mercedes from her early morning dialysis, Beth gives me a tour of the parts of the house I haven't seen. Besides the large living/dining room, sizeable kitchen, and spacious laundry room, the main floor has a small bedroom decorated with a SpongeBob Square-Pants theme for Shontel, Beth's bedroom, one large bathroom, and a large bedroom with two cribs: one for Jeffrey and one for Jaytee. A crib with a zippered net tent for a four year old seems extreme, but it makes Jaytee feel secure, even though he destroyed the zipper within two days. His crib is filled with things he sleeps with: a mostly deflated Mylar balloon, several stuffed animals, two action figures, and a tiny truck. His lack of impulse control might take the form of trying to go escape during the night, so his window has been fitted with a special lock.

On the exterior wall of the laundry room, Beth points out a wide door I hadn't noticed. It opens to a ramp leading down to the driveway. Although none of the kids currently in the house use a wheel chair, this would be the entrance for a chair-bound child, and I am reminded that kids with different medical or physical challenges have lived here throughout the years.

A stairway off the kitchen leads downstairs. Midway down is a door to a large backyard that has a high wood fence surrounding swings, a covered sandbox, and several large Tonka trucks and other toys. Because it's early spring in the Northwest, this is not the backyard it will be in late spring, summer, and fall. But it still appeals to the kid in me.

At the bottom of the stairway, stand the important second refrigerator and a substantial freezer. Four bedrooms provide private spaces for the older family members. Markie's bedroom door is covered in netting and pictures of people and animals. David's room is Spartan and tidy. His exercise equipment sits in one corner ready for part of his twice-daily workouts. Mercedes's room stands in stark contrast: Clothes, books, random papers, stuffed animals, shoes and purses are scattered across the room leaving little room to walk around. Of more interest to me are her water color paintings and pencil drawings which not only cover the walls but are strewn across all horizontal surfaces. Coleen's room is locked. When I express concern about getting a partially deaf girl's attention in an emergency when she's behind a locked door, Beth explains that she has a key that can unlock all the bedroom doors, and that, as a young adult in a full house, Colleen's privacy matters. Beth points out the intercom outside the bedrooms; and the smoke alarms which have blinking lights for Coleen and any other children who might be hearing impaired.

Finally, there is a huge walk-in closet. Even though the house is full of people, I am a bit astonished by the three floor-to-ceiling shelves chock full of children's clothes, but before I have a chance to ask any questions, it is time to go.

The tour over, we leave to pick up Mercedes at the hospital, so Coleen takes charge of Jeffrey. David is making himself breakfast as we say good bye. I silently scold myself for doubting his self-sufficiency.

As we drive, Beth talks about Coleen, her adopted daughter. When Coleen and her twin sister were born prematurely they remained in the hospital for months. The twin sister was the stronger of the two and her parents took her home while Coleen remained hospitalized. She never joined her biological family. As unimaginable as this sounds, and perhaps because it seems inconceivable, Beth offers no details about what happened to that family, but continues to tell me more about Coleen. When she was released from the hospital, this tiny deaf infant came to Beth's house on Sylvia Street, where she joined David, also adopted, and Beth's three biological children. Beth muses as we drive, "Deafness is an incredible disability. Conversation in the car has always been impossible. I can't look at her so she can see my face when I'm driving, and I can't sign! The rest of us learn so much and connect so much with random car conversations." I think back to the conversation that Shontel and Beth were having yesterday in the van regarding the sadness of leaving. I think of all the jokes, stories, explanations, plans, and feelings I've shared with my own children while in the car.

When the freeway takes us across a bridge that affords a glorious view, we hear and see a small plane crossing the wide expanse of blue sky. Beth points to it as an example. "I'm thinking Coleen doesn't realize how many planes are in the sky. Usually, we hear a plane and then look up. Since she doesn't hear them, she doesn't look up. There are a million details of life like that."

Coleen went through school in specialized classes for the hearing impaired, staying an extra year after she completed twelfth grade. After graduation, she started a job training class and received counseling, but her fragile health, frequent bouts of pneumonia, and her reticence to be out in the world both worked against her, and she quit going less than two months into the year. Her shyness prevents her from seeking out the deaf young adult community, and at twenty-four, her world remains, for the most part, Sylvia Street. "I want a larger world for Coleen," Beth says with sympathetic frustration. For now she's another adult in the house, and works willingly and competently as an assistant for Beth.

When we arrive at the dialysis center, Mercedes is done for the day. This procedure, which last three to four hours, happens three times a week for her. Her blood is circulated through an artificial kidney machine in order to filter waste and extra fluid, since her kidneys can no longer perform that function. It is not an optional procedure, since the buildup of waste and fluid can be life threatening. Mercedes is exhausted, so we stay just long enough for the nurse can share the chart numbers from Monday's printout with Beth. The nurse gently reminds Mercedes to bring her laptop on Friday; the hospital teacher had been by, and will work with her on her algebra during her next dialysis.

Today, Mercedes is not the perky, snappily-dressed teenager she was yesterday morning. She's a tired young woman in flannel pajama bottoms, a sweatshirt, and wool hat. The dialysis, plus the lupus itself, zaps her energy. She's also ravenously hungry, so Beth offers her something to eat.

After we take Mercedes home, she sleeps until it's time for the next appointment. Beth and I head for a make-up line dancing class at the community center which is humming with activity. We weave our way down the hall through preschoolers, swimmers, seniors, and artists.

Back home, Beth feeds Jeffrey, who is able to keep half of his bottle down. Drowsy now, he takes an afternoon nap. A short time later, we need drive Mercedes to the hospital for an EEG procedure to rule out seizures as the reason for her left-leg problems. Coleen will watch Jeffrey, and then walk over to the school to pick up Shontel.

At the hospital, Mercedes is still tired, and dozes as the technician measures, marks, and then glues over twenty wires to her head with a sharp and pungent smelling glue he compares to model airplane adhesive. The smell almost drives me from the room.

"Uh, could we please turn off that really obnoxious cartoon that is blaring in our ears?" Beth asks. The technician seems relieved to turn off the TV. Despite the odor of the glue, the sudden drop in noise makes the room less tense.

The wires he attaches feed into a small recording box that rests in a small attractive Jansport backpack. "Can I keep the backpack?" Mercedes inquires. The pack is the only nice thing about this whole procedure.

"Nope. We need it for other kids." He wraps Mercedes's head in gauze, and we leave for home. The battery-run box will record brain activity for 24 hours.

When we arrive at the house, Coleen takes one look at Mercedes and says, "You look weird!"

"Have you had brain surgery? Markie asks.

Mercedes is even quieter than usual. She doesn't answer or respond to the comments. I expect her to go to her room, but inexplicably, she curls up to read on the couch right in the middle of everything. Despite her dislike of babies and young children, she chooses to be in the room with the Jeffrey, Coleen, David, Markie, Daisy and the TV. She's a complicated young woman. She opens her book but mostly dozes. David stands behind her and spends several minutes staring at the glued wires. I can tell he wants to touch them, but wisely, does not.

We go pick up Jaytee from Head Start. He hasn't ripped his pants today, but on the way home he says, "Mom, I'm sad."

"Why are you sad?" Beth asks.

"I pooped my pants today." he answers.

"Okay, we'll change them when we get home." Beth answers softly. Nothing more is said about it. She changes the topic and asks him if he saw any bugs today when he was playing outside.

When we return home, Beth immediately changes Jaytee as promised, and then Coleen takes him outside to play. The boy has boundless energy. Jeffrey toddles around the living room, still coughing, and acts only slightly frustrated that a gate blocks his access to the kitchen, because the living room has the dog, Shontel, David and Markie.

After about thirty minutes, Coleen insists that Jaytee come inside. He ran into the street twice and tried to climb over the high fence in the back yard. Now he is wild with frustration, running from door to door, and trying to climb out a window.

Markie deals with his manic behavior by trying to talk over him. "I think I should cut my hair. I don't really like this TV show all that much. I think it's sort of old fashioned. I think I should get some new pencils. The ones I have don't have erasers anymore." Her free-association monologue continues. No one in the living room seems to be paying attention, and she seems to neither notice nor care.

From the kitchen, however, a slightly frazzled Beth calls out, "Markie, will you please end the nonstop chatter for just a little while!" Markie is not offended; it is as if she were just reminded that she tends to ramble. She promptly goes silent and plops down on the floor next to Daisy.

❧

TONIGHT'S MAIN COURSE is beef and vegetable stir-fry over noodles. While Beth prepares this dish, I chop the salad ingredients. When it's almost dinner time, Beth calls to Mercedes. Each night it's her responsibility to set and clear the table. I bring another chair, and adjust the others so they will all fit at the table. For a brief moment this confuses David, so I explain that since I'm an extra person, we'll need another chair.

By bending down face to face and talking quietly, Beth gets Jaytee to focus on dinnertime, and to realize that he is hungry. He settles down, and we all sit down to eat. Mercedes, who is sitting next to me, offers me her salt-free Mrs. Dash for my stir-fry.

"It's not bad", she says.

I try it, while David and Markie, sitting at my end of the table, watch me with interest. David decides he'll try a tiny bit of it, too. He wrinkles his nose at the taste. Markie considers this for a moment, and then decides to get the teriyaki sauce from the kitchen. She puts it on her stir fry and offers it to me.

"No thanks," I respond. "I'm not much a fan of the sugary stuff."

"Oh, that's why I like it," she says laughing. "I love sugar!"

After dinner Jaytee gets a bath. He loves bath time, and plays in the tub for a long time. Afterward, Beth turns on the TV hoping to watch a few minutes of a basketball game while she plays with Jeffrey in her lap, but it turns out the there's only a minute left before half time. More of her attention goes to Jeffrey, who giggles and snuggles his head in her chest.

Shontel grabs a book of fairy tales for beginning readers and climbs up on the arm of Beth's chair. She and Shontel take turns, each reading a page. They laugh together at the funny parts and talk about the pictures. As they read, she gradually leans closer and closer to Beth. When Shontel comes to a word she doesn't know, she calls it a 'hot word'. Beth gives her a little time to work it out, and then reads the word if Shontel can't.

"What a great reader you are!" I tell her, and she has trouble hiding a smile. She seems slightly awkward with the praise.

Markie, playing on the floor with Daisy, pipes up happily: "Yeah, she reads better than me!"

Coleen helps a clean and calm, well, calmer Jaytee put on his pajamas. He then plays for thirty minutes or so with a damp washcloth. He wipes the dining room chairs, the arms of the couch and the easy chair, and then he discovers the windows. Standing on a chair or the couch, he "washes" all the windows he can reach. Mercedes is curled up on one end of the couch reading and napping. Jaytee climbs over her to get to the windows behind the couch.

Beth coaxes: "Jaytee, move away from Mercedes. Go wash different windows. Clean these over here."

If Mercedes noticed that he was climbing around next to her wired head, she did a good job of ignoring it. No one minds what he's doing. It's not destructive. The worst that can happen is that the windows will need de-smudging.

David is making himself some dessert, a one-serving pudding cake called Warm Delights. After water is added, he will need to microwave it. David brings the package into the living room, and kisses Beth on the side of the head.

"I love you, Mom" he says. "How much water?"

Beth reads the package directions. "One tablespoon and one teaspoon."

"How much numbers?" David asks.

Beth knows what he means. "Forty seconds."

"Is that the four and then the zero and then the start?" he checks.

She nods, and resumes reading with Shontel.

David returns a few minutes later with the measuring spoons. "Which is the tablespoon and which is the teaspoon?"

She shows him. I marvel at her patience as she listens to the beginning reader sounding out words and simultaneously helps David, who wants to make himself dessert,

Several minutes, much more than forty seconds later, David carries his warm chocolaty dessert to the computer and finds Sprout, a PBS website for kids that features games and videos. He switches back and forth between Sprout and, inexplicably, because he can't really read, a site showing episodes of Wheel of Fortune. He shares his dessert with Jaytee, who takes a break from "washing" every few minutes for a bite.

Shontel decides she's hungry and asks for a bedtime snack. Beth suggests she get it herself since Jeffrey needs to be fed a bottle. Shontel, using a stool, gets a bowl, the cereal, and the gallon of milk and brings them to the table. She eats her snack and returns everything to where it belongs.

Markie asks Beth if she thinks it was okay for one of her classmates with diabetes to eat a frosted cupcake that another classmate had brought as a birthday treat for the class to share. Beth compliments Markie on her concern, but she cautions her about telling others what to do. "Maybe let the teacher handle that, okay?"

By the time Shontel and Jaytee have finished brushing their teeth, Jeffrey has finished his bottle and has fallen asleep in Beth's arms. She puts him to bed and snuggles a few minutes with a now-tired Jaytee, before putting him in bed, too. Shontel climbs into Beth's lap and sits for a short while cuddling and sucking her two middle fingers. Then she gets a goodnight hug and takes herself to bed.

Mercedes has been tired all evening. Beth coaxes her to the table for a blood pressure reading, a snack, and an evening dose of meds. She talks with the girl about whether she's had any trouble with her leg this afternoon and makes some notes about what she has eaten today. Mercedes wants Beth to buy some pizza rolls and frozen burritos, but Beth reminds her that her dietary restrictions make most frozen snack food off limits. It hasn't been that long since Mercedes has been out of the hospital, and like choosing items from a restaurant menu, learning how to make appropriate food choices for herself at home is something new.

Beth suggests some alternatives. "How about you cut some potatoes tomorrow morning and put them to soak for eight hours to release the potassium? Then we can make baked French fries tomorrow night." Potassium level is just one of the many issue for those with kidney failure, and potatoes have too much potassium for her system.

"Okay." It's not pizza rolls, but she's game.

Markie says goodnight and takes Daisy down to her bedroom. Once Mercedes has prepared for bed, Beth attaches the pump standing next to her bed to a small port in the girl's abdomen. It will slowly provide nutrition and medication to her throughout the night. The pump is necessary at this point because her body cannot handle too much fluid or too many calories at one time, and spreading her intake over twenty-four hours, rather than just her waking hours, is easier on her body.

Driving back to the hotel, I think about the whirlwind day. In the elevator up to the second floor, I think about Jaytee wanting to push the buttons. Walking down the hall to my room, I think about how much David would love vacuuming this long expanse of carpet. I think about lupus and dialysis and fetal alcohol exposure and lifelong complications from prematurity. Another foster mom once told me that some kids have a hard body to live in. When I get back to the hotel, I check my email. Today's message from a quote-of the-day email from a friend is a C.S. Lewis quote: "You don't have a soul, you are a soul. You have a body." Could there have been a better quote to end that particular day at Sylvia Street?

THE DINING ROOM –
THE DINNER HOUR

DID YOU EAT dinner at the table with your family when you were a kid? What about now? Does the call for dinner sound like, "Everybody into the car!"? For several years there have been public service announcements on television touting the value of a family dinner hour. Studies by Harvard and by the National Center on Addiction and Substance Abuse of Columbia University have backed up the benefits of a family dinner hour, with statistics related to lower rates alcohol, drug, and tobacco use among kids. These children also tend to have fewer incidents of depression and suicide, increased academic success, and a more advanced vocabulary.

Maybe Beth didn't read those studies. As a kid, though, she dreamed of a table full of family at dinnertime, and you can see a dream fulfilled when she sits at the head of the table most nights a week. David, the oldest young adult in the house, sits opposite Beth. Jeffrey sits close by in his high chair, even though eating anything will be sketchy at best. Shontel and Jaytee sit in youth chairs on either side of Beth. The rest fill in the other chairs. I can tell by the calm demeanor that it's a comforting ritual for those gathered around. Faces are relaxed. Voices are softer than before dinner.

The meal happens because Beth cooks. Mercedes sets and clears the table every night, without much reminding or complaint. In addition to dishes, silverware, cloth napkins, and glasses, she puts a pitcher of water and a gallon of milk on the table. As serving dishes are filled, she carries them from the kitchen to the dining room.

It usually takes a few minutes to get everyone to the table. Jaytee may be excited about something else, David may be focused on something else, and Coleen may not have heard that it's dinnertime. Nobody eats until everyone has gathered. Beth then leads the family in one of two simple graces: either "Our hands we fold. Our heads we bow. For food and drink we thank you now. Amen" or "Come, Lord Jesus; be our guest. Let this food to us be blessed. Amen." Grace is both spoken and signed. Jaytee always signs the "Amen"; even Baby Jeffrey does some hand motions. Beth serves the little ones, and the older ones pass the serving dishes to each other. Then they eat. Frequently Jaytee spills food or his milk. Markie often needs some kind of dressing or sauce that isn't on the table and jumps up to get it. Maybe Mercedes is too exhausted to eat much. Perhaps David has an aversion to a particular food. Nonetheless, it's a dinner hour and a conversation. It happens five or six nights a week.

Beth says that many kids coming to her house have not partici-pated in family dinners at the table and have rarely tasted fresh fruit and vegetables, seafood, or spices. Asparagus and artichokes are new taste experiences. Food prepared from scratch is often a new expe-rience. Except for Mercedes, those currently eating at Beth's table have done so since they were very young. Those who have come and gone in years past, whose school photos parade across the top of the high shelf in the corner, had, while they lived here and ate around this big table, a chance to develop a new appreciation for good food.

The conversation is wide ranging.

Markie pipes up: "I wish I could someday ride in a limousine like that sick boy got to do." It was a wish-fulfillment for a very ill child.

"You're not sick." Beth reminds her.

"Oh, that's right."

"Mom, when is the church garage sale?" David wants to pack or organize donations.

"Next fall. We've got time."

Shontel would rather eat in silence and follow the conversation with her eyes, but answers Beth's questions what kind of cupcakes she'd like to take to school on the last day before she moves.

"Chocolate."

Mercedes is quiet, but don't miss one bit of the conversation. Her eyebrows react to what she hears. Jaytee is generally oblivious, but appears comforted by the routine. Coleen misses much of what is said, yet seems to feel comfortable in the moments of socialization, and Beth makes sure to include her with signing and speaking directly to her. One night Jeffrey tries out melt-in-your-mouth finger food and throws up in his high chair. No one is fazed except Markie, who immediately vocalizes her disgust. Beth cleans up the mess, as well as Jaytee's spilled milk, without losing her cool.

"Mom, do you think the bathroom waste basket need to be emptied?" This is David's way of announcing that he is done with dinner.

"Yes, David, go ahead."

As people finish, Mercedes clears plates for those too young to do it themselves. Markie empties and loads the dishwasher in addition to clearing and cleaning the counters. David wipes off the table and cleans the floors. It's not exactly clockwork, but close to it.

During the years when David and Coleen were children, Beth hired college students, especially those in nursing programs, to help her during the dinner hour, bath time, and bedtime. I think about the contributions they would have made to the dinner hour conversations. I remember learning about Alily's growth in English during the time she lived with Beth, and how vital dinnertime would have been, and consider the sponge that is Shontel's mind, soaking up the conversations around her. Baby Jeffrey's speech is delayed, but how wonderful that he has this exposure to conversation around the big oval table every night. They're not talking politics or pondering philosophies, but they are sharing, and worrying, and wondering, as a family.

DINING ROOM – THE OFFICE

When it's not meal time, the expansive dining table provides a place for Beth to manage, often using her nursing skills, the paperwork, phone calls, and emails of her caseload. She sits with a giant three-ring notebook divided into sections for each child or young adult in her home. Her wireless phone has a head set so she can listen hands-free without a speaker broadcasting to the room. Her iPad sits next to the notebook.

Each week there might be medical, dental, or counseling appointments to make, contacts with teachers or tutors to schedule, and prescriptions and medical equipment to order. She often communicates with social workers, biological parents if they are in the picture, upcoming adoptive parents, and tutors, as well as organizations like Child Protective Services and the Department of Developmental Disabilities. For new children in the household, there might be calls for enrollment in school, Head Start, or swimming and music lessons. Maybe she arranges transportation for Coleen or David to an appointment or gathering. Since neither can drive, they both qualify for subsidized rides provided by the state for disabled adults.

It was undoubtedly at this table that she researched Hmong customs and beliefs in order to provide appropriate care for one of her former foster children. The Northwest has Hmong communities in several major cities. They first arrived in the United States in the 1970's when war destroyed their Laotian mountain lifestyle.

American Hmong communities in this part of the country are a blend of traditional and nontraditional lifestyles. People have close ties with their particular clan, and while education and jobs have moved them in some ways into the mainstream of American life, many families have maintained their language and cultural values. Several years ago Beth cared for a Hmong baby with diabetes insipidus, a rare condition that renders the body unable tolerate sodium and therefore unable to regulate fluids. Babies with diabetes insipidus often suffer from continually wet diapers, fevers, weight loss and delayed growth. While the child lived with her, Beth and the case worker were invited to the family's Sunday gatherings where special meals were prepared and the clan shaman conducted healing ceremonies for the child. In this case the parents had neither abandoned nor mistreated their child. Rather, their poor English and limited exposure to Western medicine, and more significantly, perhaps, the economic impossibility of staying home with a sick child or hiring a full time nurse made it impossible for them to care for their baby.

In addition to learning about other cultures, Beth has spent much time at this table working with other medical foster moms to advocate for policy changes and streamline procedures. This is also the place where she set up monthly dinners where the women can meet to support each other and, as a group, try to exert their influence on the foster-care bureaucracy.

The dinner table is also where Beth manages finances. When I tell people about her, they often say things like, "All those foster kids? Wow! Do you know how much money she must make?" If only that were true. She receives less than $500 a month for Jaytee, Shontel, and Markie. That's $1500. For Mercedes and Jeffrey, the more medically fragile children: maybe $800 each. That totals $3100 a month. The contributions from David's and Coleen's SSI together add another $600 for a total of $3700 a month. When you consider the sacrifices Beth makes to care for these children, this amount seems paltry. She has no employee benefits: no sick leave, no vacation pay, no employer retirement fund, and no bonuses. Her work is not considered self-employment, so she cannot pay into social security. She purchased the two vans with her own money and pays her own car insurance. Perhaps most strikingly, Beth's workday does not end at five, nor does she have the weekends free to recuperate. She shoulders her responsibilities twenty-four hours a day, seven days a week. How could anyone think she makes a lot of money, or has a lot of time to spend it?

All that said, this is also the same table where she makes reservations for the whole Sylvia Street household to go the beach for a week in the summer. It's where she reserves library books for herself on line, because although her days seem too full to add anything else, she's a voracious reader, and in a world of continual medical appointments, with lots of waiting, there is time to read.

Thursday

When I arrive at Beth's house, a case worker is picking up Jeffrey for his morning of supervised visits with his parents. Who knows if these visits will lead to a reunification of the family? Beth is not optimistic that this will be the case. The parenting classes are not going well, and Jeffrey's mom and dad routinely ignore the restraining order that prohibits contact between them. At the supervised visits, Jeffrey's mother has trouble managing Jeffrey and his younger sibling at the same time. She also frequently misses her scheduled visits. In light of all this, the judge has asked that two possible futures be planned: either reunification with the parents or adoption, hopefully by a relative. This two-fold planning is not unusual in the world of foster care. The goal is to have children returned to their parents, but a plan B must be in the works if the judge feels reunification might not be possible.

Until then, it's business as usual at Sylvia Street, and Jeffrey is not the only one with a busy day. Markie is working today, under supervision, at a waffle stand as part of her post high school vocational training. Beth has already started the first load of wash and has cleaned Mercedes's nighttime pump. She sits down at the dining table to order medical supplies and prescription refills and speak with Jaytee and Shontel's caseworker about the weekend plans when the adoptive mom will arrive from out of state to meet the children. She takes a call from Mercedes's case worker, who will in the next hour travel to the girl's hometown for a hearing on Mercedes's care. These hearings happen on a regular basis to check the appropriateness of a child's foster placement. Because of scheduled medical appointments, neither Beth nor Mercedes can attend the meeting, so Beth updates the case worker on Mercedes's current health and school status.

Beth explains to me that she is not always consulted when these procedures are scheduled. She prefers to attend if she can, and if it's not possible or appropriate to bring the child being discussed, she likes to take photos, so that they remember they're talking about a specific child. She sighs and begins to tell me about Mercedes's background. She lived with her dad, who had disabling health problems of his own. She was in some ways his caretaker as a preteen. Her mom was not in the picture.

"When her dad was arrested for drug dealing, Mercedes moved in with his ex-girlfriend." she says with a sigh and an eye roll. "That woman was actually designated a foster mom." In theory, living with someone you know is a good thing, but her health needs were ignored in this household, too.

When Mercedes became very sick and needed to be hospitalized, doctors discovered that she had lupus. It's not clear how long she had had this chronic auto-immune disease, since it is a rascal of an illness to diagnose with flares and remissions. Some young people may have fevers, rashes, or kidney involvement, but not necessarily. The disease is tricky to identify under the best of circumstances, but the girl's health care had been spotty at best. For example, she had never been to the dentist, and arrived at Sylvia Street with fourteen cavities. Her first dental appointment is next month. Unnoticed and untreated, lupus can wreak havoc. A person's body can mistake its own healthy tissue for a foreign organism or virus, and cause destruction of the joints, the skin, the blood, or the kidneys. Regular blood tests for a patient, once the disease is identified, can spot early signs of tissue or organ damage, and treatment can help mitigate the inflammation in the affected area of the body. (Medical intervention cannot cure lupus.) Many children with lupus have kidney complications called lupus nephritis. In Mercedes's case, the disease destroyed her kidneys. It's possible that her symptoms and the damage to her body are worse because she wasn't receiving regular health care.

According to the Lupus Foundation of American, perhaps a million and a half Americans have lupus, perhaps more. It strikes mostly young women or women in their childbearing years, but also children. While it can attack people of any race, women of color are two to three times more likely to develop it. Mercedes, a young woman of color, fits the pattern.

To further complicate matters, Mercedes developed a case of cryptococcus meningitis, which infected the lining of her brain. The disastrous combination of lupus and meningitis meant hospitalization in the city. Her father never made the one-hour trip to see her. The ex-girlfriend/foster mom didn't visit either, despite repeated promises. The state then appointed Beth as a foster mom, and for the almost five months that the girl was hospitalized, it was only Beth who came to see her.

Some parents might figure out how to visit their hospitalized child from a town an hour from the city or take them for dialysis three times a week. It might mean that in a two-parent family one parent quits work. Or maybe a grandparent or other extended family member steps up to the plate. Some families arrange to stay in the city or drive back and forth every day. Social services can help with that when people are willing. In this case, the dad and the ex-girlfriend were unable or unwilling. Her father's visits since Mercedes has been at Beth's house have been minimal, and he has not been a communicative nor emotionally involved parent. Mercedes holds on to a longing for connection to her father. In her bottom drawer are Christmas gifts for him, purchased months ago. She has not had a chance to give him these gifts.

She doesn't want Beth to refer to herself as the foster mom. "Can't you just say you're Beth?" Mercedes has asked. Beth has suggested that she refer to herself as Mercedes's guardian. All that said, it is clear to me that Mercedes and Beth have a bond. Of course Mercedes needs Beth's medical expertise. Someone has to handle her seventeen medications a day! I notice that their shared love of books and their humor connects them.

I overhear a part of a conversation between them while waiting sitting in the hospital waiting room. "He still hasn't called." Mercedes quietly says.

"Mercedes, you have permission to acknowledge that your father's parenting behavior is very disappointing." Beth gently tells her.

⁓

AFTER BETH FINISHES updating Mercedes's caseworker, I ask if I should hire David to vacuum and wash my car. He's been hinting that he wants to since I arrived. I ask her how much to pay him, and she says several one dollar bills will mean more to him than a five, a ten, or a twenty. When he sits down to eat a bowl of breakfast cereal, I ask him.

"David, do you want to clean my car?"

He drops the spoon into the bowl. He's clearly thrilled. "I could vacuum the inside, and I could wash it, and I could wax it!"

I tell him the car will be in the driveway all day. He picks up his spoon and begins to eat again. He has a job for the day, but first things first.

"Mom, where's the newspaper?"

"It's already in the recycling. Oh, this is the day with the ad, right?"

He goes and pulls it out. One page interests him: a full-page ad for a shop that sells vacuum cleaners. How did he know that Thursday's paper would have a full page ad for that store? I don't know, but the ad holds his attention while he eats his cereal. Although he cannot read well, he can recognize some of the brand names in the ad.

Meanwhile Coleen has walked to Subway for a sandwich. She won't be needed for help with Jeffrey until we leave for a lunch date and afternoon appointments. Mercedes is up and working on her laptop doing algebra or English composition homework. David has finished eating and is emptying the waste baskets and taking out the garbage and recycling. The weather is glorious today. It truly feels like spring, and sunlight is filling the house. The household has a sense of calm that makes the incredible health and heartache issues of the children and young adults seem far, far away.

As I marvel at the ordinariness of the moment, Jeffrey returns from his supervised parenting visits. After a bottle, which for once he is able to keep down, he is ready for a long nap. His cough is worse, so Beth calls to make a doctor's appointment for Friday morning. He has had pneumonia several times in his short life, and this nurse foster mom isn't taking any chances.

At noon we head for a restaurant to have lunch with three of Beth's long-time friends: a former foster mom, a retired teacher, and a nurse. We laugh and talk together for more than an hour over Mexican food. Like dance class, these lunches of camaraderie and friendship are crucial parts of Beth's life.

In early afternoon we return to the hospital so that Mercedes's wires can be removed. While we are waiting Beth tells me about a former foster child from seven years ago, now adult, who came back to visit last summer. I tell Mercedes, "Just think, in seven years, this beautiful African-American woman, without puffy steroid cheeks, will walk up to the house on Sylvia Street and say, 'Hi Beth, do you remember me?'" She smiles at the thought. It's clear that surviving to adulthood wasn't always a strong possibility for Mercedes.

On the way home we pick up Jaytee. Today there's no problem with his pants! Beth compliments him on his willingness to climb into his car seat. I sense that this isn't always the case.

When we get home, David is washing my car. He proudly shows me his vacuuming job. Shontel and Jaytee choose to play outside in the front yard under Coleen's watchful eye. Mercedes decides to take her book out on the front steps. Jeffrey plays on the floor. His cold seems worse, and his eyes have the sad look of an ill child.

Tonight's dinner will be shrimp with cheese sauce, pasta, garlic bread, and fresh fruit. While Beth cooks the homemade sauce and prepares the pasta and bread, I cut the fruit and fan it out on a platter in a colorful display. "Wow, that's fancy!" says Markie. "It looks like a party!"

Jaytee can barely contain himself at the dinner table. He is distracted from dinner several times by noises outside or a toy he spots, and is up and around the room. Beth brings him back to the table each time.

While Beth corrals Jaytee back to the table, I learn that Markie turned twenty a few weeks ago. "My birthday is in spring, but I'm kind of a Christmas baby because I came here on Christmas Eve." she says, and then adds, "I kind of have over three hundred siblings. I think of it that way." Before dinner she had opened her late birthday gift from Beth that arrived in the mail today: a phone! It's her very first phone, and she is excited beyond belief. She will spend the rest of the evening learning to use it. "I'm a little nervous about texting." She tells me. "Reading and writing are difficult for me, so I'm going to avoid that for the time being."

After dinner, the warm evening calls the others back outside. Coleen chooses to stay in the house with Jeffrey, and Beth and I sit on the porch swing to watch Shontel and Jaytee play. David begins to wax my car.

"That's special wax." Beth comments. "Volvo wax."

"Why does he have Volvo wax? I ask. Beth does not own a Volvo.

"People don't know what to buy him for Christmas, so they buy him cleaning products and car care products!" she answers with a twinkle in her eye.

WHEN THIS NEIGHBORHOOD was designed a hundred years ago, city planners started a long term experiment about neighborliness. Sylvia Street itself is narrow, with parking only on one side. The grass between the curb and the sidewalk is wide. The adjacent street has parking on both sides and a narrower strip of grass. The next street over is even wider with no grass between the curb and sidewalk. Through the years, the people on Sylvia Street have talked, played, and visited with each other more than on the other streets. Tonight is a perfect example. Markie is across the street, talking with little girls who are setting up another tea party. Three young boys have pulled a portable basketball hoop into the street and are shooting hoops. Shontel and Jaytee are playing with the five-year-old boy from next door. The people just down and across the street are sitting on their porch steps and call a hello to Beth. A young family walks past on the way to a neighborhood restaurant and chats for a moment. If David were not busy waxing my car this evening, he would probably be riding around on his trike. Beth says he knows everyone on the block, and when they see people from the neighborhood in the grocery story, he is always greeted warmly. It occurs to me that it was a stroke of luck that Ed and Beth chose a house on this particular street back in the eighties.

Soon it's twilight. Jaytee has finished "mowing" the front lawn and parking strip with his toy lawn mower. Going back and forth in even swathes, he has been at it for at least twenty minutes. I am reminded of David's fascination with vacuuming. Beth asks Shontel to bring the toys back up onto the porch. She does so, making several trips, but she's complaining the whole time about being overworked.

"Why do I have to do all the work around here? I do everything." She complains.

Beth ignores her grumbling and quietly remarks, "If a kid is doing what she is supposed to be doing, you don't punish her for the attitude!"

She looks at David, and then chuckling, says to me, "You may have a polka dot car in the morning. It's getting dark, and a legally blind man is buffing your car." We both laugh.

Inside, everyone is getting cleaned up and ready for bed. Shontel has a bath and Jaytee is beside himself because he wants to get into the bathtub, too. Beth helps him into his pajamas, but he strips them off and tries to open the bathroom door. Again Beth helps him into his pajamas, and he strips them off again. Frantically, he climbs up on a chair to get a fork so he can pry the door open. When Beth stops him and gets him back into his pajamas, he climbs up onto the counter, in an effort to reach the place where he knows scissors are kept. Beth is now feeding Jeffrey a bottle, so I walk over to Jaytee to distract him.

In his ear, I whisper, "We're not getting scissors now, but I can show you how my watch face lights up. I can also read to you. Come on over here."

Amazingly, he agrees, mostly because of the watch face, which he lights up over and over again. Exhaustion and his evening medication begin to slow him down, and he actually snuggles with me for just a few minutes to look at a book of farm animals and equipment. He knows the words for *hay baler* and *combine*, but doesn't know *lamb, chick, calf,* or other animal words. Abruptly, he abruptly hops down from my lap, crawls up into his crib, and is asleep within minutes.

While Beth ties Shontel's hair into a do-rag for the night, they look at the pictures her future adoptive mom has sent. There's one of the house, an exterior view, one of the local swimming pool, and one of the mom and her two adopted daughters taken during the Christmas holidays. They appear to be in Scandinavian folk-wear.

Two other people, also in costume, are in the photo, but are not identified. After Shontel is in bed, Beth tells me that usually kids get lots of pictures of their new life: new school, bedrooms, the back yard, the family pets, etc. Shontel's minimal collection of photos bothers her. She's also frustrated that the woman has sent no letters to Shontel or Jaytee and hasn't followed through on arrangements to talk with them by phone.

"Do you think this is going to be okay?" I ask.

"It has to be." Beth answers, but her unease with the situation is obvious.

The house is quiet now. The little ones are all asleep. Markie is entering phone numbers into her new phone, and David is watching Sprouts on the computer. Mercedes has finally washed her hair, necessary after the treatment to unglue the wires, and she and Beth now discuss baked fries. The potatoes Mercedes cut have soaked for eight hours. Beth brings a cookbook with recipes for people with kidney failure into the living room, and they sit together on the couch trying to find a good recipe. Suddenly Mercedes looks at her hands in disbelief. The polish on her fingers, but not her thumbs, has disappeared. "I didn't remove the polish!" she says. After a few puzzling minutes, we laugh when we figure out that when she was running her fingers through her hair before she washed it, the solvent to unglue her wires had dissolved the polish. Fortunately, it didn't dissolve her hair!

Around nine o'clock I leave to take my polka-dot car back to the hotel. By then, Beth and Mercedes have started the baked fries.

THE BIG CLOSET

Downstairs is a giant walk-in closet with floor-to-ceiling shelves on three walls. Clothing for babies, children, and teens are neatly stacked according to size. Some are clothes in good condition that children have outgrown. New socks and underwear in several sizes await the children who will arrive in the future, perhaps with only the clothes they are wearing.

This is not to say that the kids on Sylvia Street are raggedly dressed in hand-me-downs from the closet, in spite of the small clothing allowance provided by the state. There are private non-profit organizations in the city that provide clothing "closets" for foster kids. Area footwear manufacturers or dealers provide shoes. Beth also takes pride in how her kids look. While I was there, all of the kids were well dressed. At one point, Jaytee couldn't find his sneakers or his crocs, so he pulled out his dress shoes. How many four-year-old boys in this decade have dress shoes?

Some kids stay on Sylvia Street for years, some for weeks, some for a weekend. As a twenty-year-old, Markie has been there most of her life, but I learned that an infant was recently there for just two days. A two-month-old was released from the hospital and needed nursing care for just the weekend until the new foster mom could come and get her from a county six hours away. Beth called the infant a sweet broken baby. When she was hospitalized for meningitis, her teen father admitted that he had shaken her. The result was broken ribs, broken vertebrae, and a broken leg. Because of swelling in the brain from hematomas, a doctor drilled in her skull to relieve the pressure. Beth commented that she was a cute little baby who ate well, but that the long term prognosis regarding her head injury remains unknown.

It takes my breath away to think about the never-ending stream of medically fragile infants and children needing foster care. Many can't live with their parents because of abuse, neglect, abandonment or prison. But in some cases, Beth has nursed and nurtured children whose loving families are simply unable to navigate the medical system. When a child's medical problems have been stabilized or resolved, he or she might return home or go to a permanent adoptive home. If neither of those options is available, a child might remain on Sylvia Street. Moving to another foster home not only takes an emotional toll on a child, but also jeopardizes health gains.

Several times in the past two decades Beth cared for siblings where one child had cancer and needed nursing foster care, and the children were kept together. She explained that twice the "medical kid" died, and the siblings continued to live with her for another couple of years until they were adopted.

"Not all medical foster moms take in kids with life threatening illnesses; they don't want kids dying in their houses. But a terminally-ill child deserve a family and a home." She states passionately.

So do the grieving siblings, I think to myself. Beth could handle that.

The head of pediatric nursing in a local hospital explained to me that while she didn't have statistics, she felt that children with huge health challenges enter foster care at a higher rate than other children. There are two explanations for this. Many medically fragile children come from mothers who drink or use drugs, and they would be in foster care even if they didn't have medical issues. However, the drugs and alcohol create problems for children even before they are born. There might be increased chances of prematurity which can lead to many complications. There may be issues with brain development. Sometimes the strain of caring for a child destroys a family that is already stressed to the breaking point by poverty or dysfunction. If just one member of an intact and financially stable family has a drug or alcohol problem and has a child, the extended family might have the resources to take on the responsibility for care, and the foster care system does not get involved.

The head of social work at a local hospital told me how he is regularly amazed by the work of families with medically fragile kids: the hours of care, the scheduling, the programs, the twenty-four-seven medical needs, the unmet needs of other children in the family, the isolation that comes from limited social time, the money problems as a result of time off work. It takes its toll. What happens if the family is not strong and stable to begin with? The social worker said that in his hospital, for various reasons, two or three children a week are released to a foster parent with at least some medical training. Occasionally, a parent just walks away. Sometimes a child is hospitalized longer than is ideal until a caretaker is found.

I asked a friend who works as an advocate for the disabled, "What happens to children if people like Beth aren't available?"

"Sometimes they die, Judy." she answered softly. A child needs more than adequate medical care to thrive.

Every now and then, however, the story is breathtakingly tender. Consider ten-year-old Roxie, Beth's former foster child we ran into at the counseling center. She had come to live with Beth as a baby due to complications from a premature birth. An adoption by a single man was in the works. But then, while still a toddler, Roxie developed leukemia. The adoptive dad could not handle the financial expense of treating the leukemia. If he adopted her, Roxie's medical expenses would still be covered, but not the cost of hiring a nurse nor time off from work to care for the girl. The soon-to-be dad waited in the wings and developed a relationship with his soon-to-be daughter. Later, she was healthy enough that he was able to become her foster dad, and she moved away from Sylvia Street. When Roxie was six, and cancer free, the adoption was finalized. Beth attended the ceremony at the courthouse, and recalled affectionately that the father, who had stood by Roxie through the illness and kept his commitment to adopt her, cried.

THE LIVING ROOM – COMCAST AND THE SOCK MONKEY FAREWELLS

A COUCH AND *two large comfortable chairs with a lamp table between them line two walls of the living room, yet there is still enough space on the floor for little ones to toddle or play with toys and big ones to stretch out to watch a program or play with the dog. The television has a giant screen, and because of Coleen's hearing loss, always has captions displayed.*

A man working for the TV cable service in the neighborhood was doing an installation a few years ago when he recognized David riding his trike. Realizing he was near Sylvia Street, the man walked up to the door and knocked. "Hi, Beth. I used to live here ten years ago!" he said. Although he didn't give her any hints to help her remember, she was able to recall that he and his sister, who had leukemia, had lived with her for several years.

While his visit was serendipitous, many grown foster kids intentionally stay in contact or reestablish contact with Beth. For example, Katya called last summer and arranged a visit, bringing her own two-year old child. Beth had been a lifesaver for Katya. For years she and her three sisters had been living in a car with their mom, but when Katya developed diabetes, the challenges of home-lessness and disease management were an impossible combination. Two former foster sisters with whom she had reconnected through

Facebook visited as well. That comfortable living room served as an informal reunion site.

Social networking has allowed former foster kids to reconnect. In addition to Katya, other young adults who lived with Beth have reconnected with each other and with her because of that tool. Likewise, cells phones and texting have allowed some young adults, like Alily, to stay in contact. Alily, whose platelet disorder is under control, lives with her own family again.. When her health allows it, she comes back to Sylvia Street to not only visit, but also to occasionally work for pay as a babysitter or do light housekeeping chores.

What happens when foster children turn eighteen? Current regulations are changing in the Northwest, but most physically healthy young adults who have been in the foster care system go out into the world alone. Funding ends. Stories abound of young people untethered and disconnected from their communities. In Vanessa Diffenbauch's novel The Language of Flowers, the dramatic and stark reality of aging out of foster care is movingly described, as Victoria, the main character, ages out of foster care and ends up sleeping in a park with everything she owns.

The young adults in Beth's house are the exception to the norm. Coleen and David were adopted as children, so they didn't leave.

Markie's disabilities allow her to stay in foster care until she is twenty-one, but it will be impossible for her to live independently, so she'll eventually move to a foster care home for adults or a group home that provides sheltered housing for adults. Many young adults with Fetal Alcohol Syndrome/Evidence and a higher IQ run into trouble with the law. The statistics would suggest more than half of them. Perhaps Markie's low IQ is a blessing. She will remain in sheltered care. I suspect that her Christmases will be spent on Sylvia Street, sitting cross legged on the floor in front of the fireplace with her dog.

౿〇

THE COMFORTABLE RECLINER *in the living room is the perfect place to cuddle a little one or watch a Chicago Bulls game, but perhaps most importantly, it's the place to embroider eyes on a sock monkey. One of the first things I learned about Beth's work is that she gives each child a handmade sock monkey when they leave Sylvia Street. I watched her sewing the eyes on one during a class reunion several years ago. When I got home from my visit to Sylvia Street, I emailed Beth and asked her if she had sent sock monkeys with Jaytee and Shontel when they moved. She responded with an email that told me about their last weekend and said that, yes, she had tucked sock monkeys into their backpacks. She added that she didn't sob in front of them when they left.*

Jaytee and Shontel's last few days at Beth's house were difficult ones. Although Jaytee is a cheerful boy most of the time, he is never easy, and athough he could not talk about the stress of a life-changing event, he acted out, and his behavior was especially difficult. The emotional sadness of saying goodbye and the excitement of finally being adopted wore on all three of them.

Shontel entered the foster care system when she was quite young, in part due to domestic violence. She was challenged by speech and language problems and extreme tantrums. When her substance-abusing biological mother gave birth prematurely to Jaytee two years later, one of his health issues was the inability to eat. For several weeks he was fed through a tube. When he came to Beth's house, he learned to take a bottle in four days. Beth's comment was, "A committee can't teach a baby to eat".

Four years later Jaytee has a hale and robust body, but his language and problem solving skills resemble that of a two-year-old. His impulsivity and occasional rages are truly remarkable. He's a perpetual motion machine whose energy could light up a small town. How many of Jaytee's challenges are due to prenatal drug and alcohol exposure? How much is inherited from a mom who self-medicated because she had the same challenges?

The state works to keep siblings together in foster care, so Shontel joined her brother at Sylvia Street. When she started kindergarten, it became clear that an attention deficiency and hyperactivity syndrome were interfering with her ability to learn. With medication, her first grade year has been a different story, and her learning has outpaced expectations as she's become a strong reader.

The two children have been available for adoption for several years, but understandably, placement for these two has not been easy. What potential parent asks for a hyperactive six-year-old with a raging brother who behaves like a toddler? Shontel, on the other hand, had a request: She told Beth she wanted a family with a dad.

More than a year ago, social services found a potential adoptive family. A couple from the rural Midwest, they belonged to a very conservative religious sect, and planned to give the children biblical names. They expected Shontel to wear a long cotton dress and headscarf. A rough and tumble child, she was most interested in the photos of the barn and the fields of her home to be, and not so interested in the picture of a canopied, ruffled bed waiting for her. She told her counselor that when she was adopted, she was going to become a little white farm girl named Esther.

When the family came for a visit, it was alarmingly clear to Beth and Shontel's counselor that the emotional and physical well-being of Shontel-to-be-Esther and Jaytee-to-be-Jeremiah could be in serious jeopardy. It was obvious that the couple did not want to adopt kids with personalities, names, likes, and dislikes, but rather blank people that they could shape and form to make the children they wanted. They refused to take any of the children's favorite toys or possessions. They weren't interested in hearing about Jaytee's developmental challenges or Shontel's hyperactivity. That adoption was stopped at the last minute officials were made aware of the many signs of a dangerous mismatch between kids and potential parents.

With mixed emotions, Beth welcomed the news that another adoptive parent was identified earlier this spring. Finally, the two *children would have a permanent family. Unfortunately for Shontel, the parent is a single mom in her 40's. No dad. Plus, the new home for these two children of color will be with a white mom and sisters in a white community in the Midwest. As Beth arranged for adoption preparation play therapy for Shontel, packed toys and clothes, and arranged for records transfer with the school and with Head Start, she did so with a little sadness, not so much because she was losing two kids she'd grown to love, but because the communication with the new mom was not reassuring. True, she wasn't changing their names or expecting them to dress in nineteenth-century clothing, but promised phone calls didn't happen. Letters didn't come. Only minimal photos arrived. There was not a flood of questions on email about the kids' likes and dislikes, quirks, needs, and foibles.*

Of course the adoption was necessary and thank goodness this woman has stepped up to the task. At age sixty-three, Beth believes she is too old to see these two children into adulthood. She would be 77 when Jaytee graduates from high school.

One night when we were alone in the living room, I asked, "How can you let them go?"

With clear eyes, she answered, "People ask that, but the fact is: I can. These two will be tough to raise. It hurts a lot for a while when they leave, but if they stay it will hurt a lot longer. Besides, this is the way the system is supposed to work. I can't help other kids if these two don't go to a new home." Later, with a wry smile, she added, "And when Jaytee's gone, I can replace the drapes in the living room that he's destroyed!"

The transition to the children's new family did not go as smoothly as planned. Beth explained that the new mom didn't show up Friday afternoon as expected because her flight was later than she had originally planned. Saturday morning Shontel was up on the couch by the front window waiting anxiously for her arrival. When the case worker and new mom arrived, Shontel ran into her bedroom and stayed there for twenty-five minutes, yelling silly things at her brother.

When Jaytee saw the caseworker, he yelled "Daddy!" Beth explained that it was the result of the man's rare five-minute visits over the last three years. Shontel could only be coaxed out of her room because it was time for swimming lessons.

The new mom accompanied them to the pool, and then came back to the house for a half hour on Saturday night and then again on Sunday evening. She never left the couch in the living room, never saw the children's rooms, and had only one question: "What do you use on Shontel's hair?"

Sunday afternoon Beth and Shontel purchased cupcakes for a farewell party at school. Monday evening the family held their own farewell party, and the kids were given their sock monkeys. When Shontel was getting in bed for the night she said to Beth, "I don't want to go on the airplane tomorrow. Do I have to go?"

She shared with me her response. "I was really glad that night that I am too old to adopt Shontel, because otherwise when she asked me why couldn't just stay with me forever, I wouldn't have been able to let her go."

Tuesday morning the children were excited about a plane ride when the caseworker and mom arrived to pick them up. A few days later Shontel called and sounded upbeat. Beth had a chance to talk to the new mom, and came away from the conversation with more positive feelings about her.

The Irish Pub, Starbucks, and the Italian Restaurant

A FEW DAYS *after I return home, I call my friend Margie. She has lived with lupus for years, and can perhaps help me understand the disease that is so hard on Mercedes's body. We agree to meet for lunch at an Irish pub near her house. In a dark wood booth, with the Chieftains playing in the background, and a soccer game on the tv above the bar, we discuss fostering and lupus and writing. I learn what a vexation lupus can be. Her flares can be triggered by something as simple as smoke or too much sun. I think about Mercedes's dental issues. Maybe even one cavity could trigger a flare. I feel for both of them. When the conversation turns to my book, Margie encourages me to talk with a published writer about the process ahead of me. "A little mentoring," she says.*

A few days later I remember that the mother of a former student of mine is a published author. I haven't talked to her in years, but she graciously agrees to meet with me at a convenient Starbucks. She even buys my latte, and gives me not only great writing advice, but a link in a chain of people that leads in a wonderful direction. A week later I'm waiting in yet another Starbucks.

Which one of these people coming in the door is a long-time foster mom? I wonder. Nobody coming through the door looks patient enough. When Susan does arrive, it is her serene and kind demeanor that I notice first.

Over the next few hours I learn about her life, her biological children, her adopted children, and the many foster children she cared for over the years. Just recently Susan retired from fostering. She and her husband adopted two medically fragile children from India who are both adults now. Her own adopted daughter, challenged by polio as a child, is married and works as a barista. Her adopted son, with a rare blood disorder, is a college student.

Susan tells me there was usually just one foster child in their house at a time, often a fetal alcohol syndrome baby or one damaged in utero by drugs. She's clearly knowledgeable and compassionate, and when I tell her about Jaytee and Shontel, she not only has an understanding of their challenges, but she further explains their behavior and offers insight about what Beth has gone through in caring for these children.

Susan has remained in contact with a little boy she cared for from infancy, now in grade school, who was adopted and lives in a nearby city. Like Jaytee, he's a bundle of energy with little self-control or executive functioning ability. She described him, and other children like him, as needing someone beside them to continually help with decision-making. Since children with these kinds of developmental issues don't always learn from experience, and often can't self-regulate, an angel on the shoulder who is whispering in the ear seems somehow essential. Weekly Susan takes him swimming, and regularly babysits for the couple. Volunteer respite care might be a better phrase to describe the time she gives.

I think about what Jaytee will be like in a few years. Similar to Susan's former foster child, he will probably need to be in a special classroom with just a few other kids, assuming he lives in a community with the academic resources to serve him. Maybe a good day will mean no fights at school, as it does for Susan's adoptive "grandson."

Before I know it, I realize we've been talking for four and a half hours! I apologize for the time.

"Don't apologize. Nobody wants to hear about the kids who require intense nurturing and over-the-top care, or about the stamina needed by foster moms," she tells me, "but because you want to hear it, I have lots to say!" Much of what she tells me helps me make sense of what I have seen on Sylvia Street, and it's woven into my understanding of Beth's children.

She quizzes me about how Beth copes. She herself has had a husband all these years, both a partner in nurturing and a man with an income. I explain that when Beth was still a child she saw herself becoming a foster mom someday. I explain her involvement in her church, her love of reading, her easy laugh. Susan talks about a purpose-driven life. She and Beth are two of a kind, I think.

Because, like Beth, she talked about great frustration with the bureaucracy, I decide that I need to talk with someone who works for the state. Through my book club connections, I arrange to meet Sam, an employee in the state foster care system.

∽⊙

I ALLOW PLENTY of time and arrive early at the Italian restaurant near the state capital with my notebook and my little audio recorder in my purse. I'm hoping he can give me the bigger picture of foster care from his vantage point in child welfare operations at the state level. When he arrives we choose a table where it will be easy to have a conversation.

"So you're writing a book," he says after we've ordered our lunch. I try not to bombard him with a million questions at once. First we talk about the numbers. About eight thousand kids are in foster care in the state at any one time. He thinks that about nineteen thousand children a year spend at least one night in care.

Over minestrone soup, we discuss poverty and foster care. He affirms what others have told me about the undeniable connection of the two, how extended families who are not poor can often take on the responsibility for a fragile child who needs parenting. Sam stresses that the need for the state to care for many children is the result of larger societal problems such as drug use, alcohol abuse, teenage pregnancy, and lack of health care.

He muses for a minute, taking a bite of his salad and thinks carefully about his words. He sets his fork down and looks me straight in the eye. "Two blocks from here, there is a Planned Parenthood office. People picket it eight hours a day. I wish all those picketers would agree to be foster parents." He picks up his fork again and continues eating. In my mind I can I hear Beth wryly commenting about what kind of foster parents the picketers would be.

The pink shirt and flowered tie he's wearing today suggest a bit of whimsy, but what he has to say is not the least bit whimsical. At one time he was a caseworker in the field, and had his own caseload of medically fragile children. Now he works at the state headquarters. He explains federal and state allocations and possible changes ahead in how fostering is funded. Some people want a different kind of accountability, block grants, performance-based allocations, or privatization of services. Privately funded foundations lobby for dramatic changes to the delivery of child welfare services. As much as the bureaucracy he's part of drives him crazy, many of the proposed changes would mean a decline in services for children, as he sees it.

Sam explains his frustration and issues with the state's computer system for reporting and tracking child welfare services. Based on his many years of experience, he shares that some social workers enter the field for the wrong reasons, hoping they can fix their own problems from childhood by fixing society, and as a result, they have a hard time with the job. He notes that changes in state regulations are going to put fewer social workers in the field. Sam acknowledges the huge need for foster families and the amazing service they provide, and he thinks most foster parents do what they do for the right reasons. Nevertheless, he tells me about the ones who "hold the state hostage," demanding more money. The analogy in my head is the last time I had cherry pie. It was delicious, but one pit and that's all I could think about. Beth says that most foster moms hate talking to the state about money, that it feels demeaning, even if they know they should, for the kids' sake as well as their own. Sam's job requires him to think about money.

A small isolated village can perhaps handle one or two needy children when elders and a caretaker step up. Caring for nineteen thousand children in need of safe homes is, on the other hand, a huge task. Obviously it takes not only loving caretakers, but also managers, site supervisors, computer technicians, legal advisors, social workers, and number crunchers. The list goes on. Our culture does not have a "village" ethic. The youngest and most fragile among us are for the most part invisible. Sam in his very visible pink shirt is part of a magnificent and messy attempt by our society to avoid the horrors of a world of Dickensian waifs.

I think about how Beth likes to show pictures of her children when she's talking with bureaucrats or decision makers. On one hand, I'm overwhelmed by the heart ache and love I see on Sylvia Street and Beth and Susan's frustration with the bureaucracy. I am equally overwhelmed by the magnitude of the problem and by the career-long passion of this man to serve the vulnerable children of this state.

MONDAY – SIX WEEKS LATER

WHEN I ARRIVE at the Beth's house Monday morning in May, the flag on the porch is one of spring flowers, and on the side of the house lilacs are in full bloom. The changes outside mirror some of the changes for the people inside. Baby Jeffrey is in his high chair, and he's actually eating! Fortunately, his bib is more than just a bib. It has long sleeves and covers his whole front. It's necessary, because he's eating thick Greek yogurt and toddler food, in this case baked vegetable crisps, with his hands. Unfortunately, he hasn't gained weight, so he's still tiny. He lost weight last month when he was sick and is just back to where he was five weeks ago. He still gets most of his nutrition from a very high-calorie formula, but now he's at least handling, if not always eating, some foods.

Beth introduces me to Trina, a new young woman in the house who is home from school today because of a bad cold. Trina is a fashionably dressed and troubled middle school girl dealing with type 1 diabetes. She must regularly check her blood sugar throughout the day, pay close attention to what and when she eats, and give herself insulin shots. Her cold has thrown off her appetite, and although she knows she has to eat, nothing appeals to her. She moves around the kitchen, checking the refrigerator and the cupboards, hoping to find some food that sounds good. Although she's not at school today because of her cold, this is a rare occurrence since moving in with Beth. Before she was taken in state custody, her school attendance was spotty, since no one at home was paying attention. Trina whines to Beth that Mercedes hasn't been sharing her computer. Beth simply says, "I'll make a note of that."

Trina is in Shontel's room, now without the SpongeBob SquarePants décor. Her own abstract paintings and pencil drawings hang on the wall above her bed. She seems comfortable talking with adults. I don't know yet how she relates to the other teens. She pretty much ignores the baby.

Coleen has a new haircut and has dyed her hair a beautiful auburn shade. I make much more an effort to have a conversation with her than I did in March, but it's still a real challenge. She tends to nod her head, acting like she understands when she actually has no clue to what I've said or asked. When Jeffrey is done eating and cleaned up, she scoops him up cheerfully, and they laugh together for a few minutes before he begins to play independently.

Jeffrey is fascinated by a plastic board with colorful stacking pegs. The toy holds his interest for perhaps twenty minutes as he stacks, rearranges, and restacks the pegs. His ability to stay focused on this thrills Beth. With all of his challenges, this bodes well for his future. His language development is another story. He still just has basically one sound. When he wants up in Beth's lap, she talks and signs to him as they snuggle to encourage his language.

Around noon we leave to drop off Mercedes for dialysis. For just today, it's an afternoon procedure to accommodate another dialysis patient. If it were always in the afternoon, perhaps she could attend school part time in the morning. After dialysis she is too tired or nauseated for school, so attending in the afternoons wouldn't work. She takes her laptop along in order to work on algebra with the dialysis center tutor, but if a complication with the dialysis catheter requires that she lay flat on her back, it limits her ability to do school work.

On the way home, we stop by the church to pick up David, who has been vacuuming and dusting. He's waiting just inside the church door, and when he sees the van, he comes out. He's clearly tired, and not very talkative. When prompted, he reports that the ladies who count money brought cinnamon rolls this morning.

Back home, Markie reports that she has good news. "Next year I get to move on to the next grade!" This will be her second year beyond regular high school, available to kids with developmental delays, with an emphasis and life skills and job training. Markie sees it as a promotion. I think, *Good for her.*

Baby Jeffrey has had a good nap and wants to laugh and play on the floor around Beth's legs as she sits on the couch. Trina's cold seems better, and she and Beth agree that she can probably go to school Tuesday. She tells Beth that she talked on the phone with her mom, who has been directed by the court attend all of the girl's medical appointments. Her mom is upset and confused about next week's schedule, Trina explains. Beth remains calm, evidencing no sign of frustration with the history of negligence and lack of concern by the mom for her daughter's precarious health, and she says that she will call the mom again and clarify.

I ride along when Beth goes to pick up Mercedes. The dialysis team and the tutor talk with Beth about the condition of the girl's catheter port, her blood pressure numbers, her sodium levels, her liters of fluid, weight, temperature, her headache, her algebra units and the status of her school credits. Beth carries away a sheaf of paperwork about her Mercedes's health. The algebra and school credit information is in her head.

ABOUT FIFTY YEARS ago, the world's first outpatient kidney-dialysis center opened in what was then called the Seattle Artificial Kidney Center. At that time, very few people qualified for the chance to use the three available machines and benefit from the life-saving and very expensive treatment. According to an article in *The Seattle Times Pacific NW Magazine*, the local medical society chose an anonymous committee to select patients. They were dubbed the "God Committee" and the "Life and Death Committee." They only chose patients with the means to pay for their own treatment. They needed to be between the ages of twenty-five and forty-five, and they could not have other illnesses. As a teenager with lupus and no financial resources of her own, she would not have been a candidate for dialysis, and as a result she would have died.

Fortunately, dialysis has come a long way. In the early seventies, lawmakers granted Medicare coverage to kidney patients. A "Life and Death Committee" was no longer needed. Today non-pr0fit and for-profit dialysis centers are widespread throughout the country and serve what *Seattle Times* writer Carol Ostrom says are roughly six hundred thousand U.S. patients.

After Beth finishes talking with the dialysis team, we head back to the house. I leave before they eat dinner, which tonight will be take-and-bake pizzas, including one that fits Mercedes's dietary restrictions and one that Markie, Coleen, and David like.

THE KITCHEN

A FEW DIRTY dishes are stacked in the kitchen sink. Beth sighs, but avoids loading them into the dishwasher. As much as it bothers her, the dishes are Markie's task, and so they will sit in the sink until she's home from school to unload the clean ones and load the dirty ones. This is a task that she should have taken care of last night or this morning. Other than that, the kitchen is clean and organized.

Like all teenagers, Mercedes, Trina, and Markie are hungry at various times during the day. In addition, Mercedes's dialysis schedule throws off her meal times and appetite, so sometimes she only feels like eating at two in the afternoon or ten at night. Trina, with her type 1diabetes, on the other hand, must regularly snack, taking in specific numbers of carbohydrates. As a result, the freezer, refrigerator, fruit bowl, and several cupboards are stocked with a variety of foods to grab and go or microwave. Even first-grader Shontel knew how to get her own snack when she lived here.

One high lockable shelf contains all the medicine. A few shelves are just for food that Coleen and David have bought with their own money. Coleen will tell Beth what she wants her to buy and the items are then deducted from her small monthly government stipend; David likes to accompany Beth to the store and push the cart. Sometimes he sees things he wants her to buy for him with his debit card. Dinners for the week are planned in advance, but she still shops at a local supermarket twice a week. Regular shopping for dairy and fresh produce is necessary. Four gallons of milk last five days on Sylvia Street.

Right now there are two gallons in the kitchen refrigerator and two more in the refrigerator in the basement. In addition, she shops at Costco about every six weeks, and restocks the basement freezer with basics like cheese, meat, and seafood as well as convenience dinners. She also refills the cupboards with nonperishables, and, of course, buys another big container of laundry detergent.

The front of the refrigerator is like that of homes all across America: magnets and tape hold up photos, drawings, cartoons, quotes, schedules, and phone numbers in a crazy quilt pattern. This month's calendar page is part of the haphazard collage. It's not the detailed calendar with all the medical and counseling appointments; that is in the three-ring binder. This one includes events that are of interest to the whole household such as birthdays, holidays, school vacations, and outings.

This is May, so Mother's Day is marked on the calendar. "Maybe," Beth suggests, "this is the hardest holiday of all. Despite the love and affection that I get from the kids, this day is an in-your-face reminder for them that they are not with their mothers". While most of her foster kids show their affection and appreciation of Beth in lots of ways, they don't express that on Mother's Day. "I understand that," she says," and it makes me sad for them."

On the side of the refrigerator is a posted schedule of each person's household chores. Many of the household day-to-day tasks like dishes, mopping, vacuuming, dusting, and recycling are handled by the teens and young adults, freeing Beth to concentrate on non-household tasks or do other jobs like cleaning the refrigerator.

All but the youngest fix breakfast for themselves. Foster kids in school qualify for free lunches, and the young adults handle their own lunches. Beth cooks dinner. Details of the routine change as kids move in or leave, but the pattern is an established one that brings a level of calm and consistency, as well as cleanliness, to the household without any sense of a nagging task master being in charge. It's not perfect of course. The sink is full of dirty dishes today, and a cracker box was returned to the cupboard empty, disappointing a hungry Trina.

THE BACKYARD

WHEN I FIRST saw Beth's backyard back in March, I assumed that it was mostly used by the young children of the house. I hadn't noticed the five long parallel clotheslines that stretch along the east side. I saw the massive wooden play structure with four swings, but hadn't paid much attention to the height of the swings. I notice now that one is a chair swing for little ones, and another is low enough to the ground for children in elementary school. However, the other two swings are high off the ground: fit for adult use.

I learn that Trina likes to swing. In fact, she feels a need to swing every day. When she first moved in with Beth, she wanted to know the location of the nearest park where there might be swings. Imagine her surprise when she learned that there were several in her new backyard. I suspect swinging is soothing to her. Trina is more complicated than she looks. She has more to deal with than just diabetes. As a response to some kind of emotional deep-seated pain, she sometimes cuts herself, not to mortally injure herself, but rather to give a focus to her pain.

David also uses the swing every day, but his swinging is different. He sings as he pumps his body through the air. Sometimes he sings snatches of songs he knows, like "The Star Spangled Banner" or "In the Garden." More often, he makes up songs, and sings about what he's feeling. Beth laughingly told me the neighbors always know what going on in the house because of David's singing. One time the lyrics were, "I don't like the new girl!" No details. Just a simple refrain.

David recently suggested to Beth that they buy a barbeque for the backyard. He thought it would be nice if he could cook hot dogs for himself. She explained that a barbeque would be dangerous with little ones around, and that if she had to be outside supervising when the barbeque was going, then she couldn't be inside keeping an eye on those in the house. "Okay," he sighed.

ANOTHER TUESDAY

I ARRIVE THE next day after breakfast to find Beth once again at her dining table office. David has been weeding in the back yard, and comes into the house to talk with Beth about the idea of putting paving stones under the clotheslines. He's happy to see me and proudly shares the news that he has bought a new lawn mower. When he goes back outside, Beth explains that it's a recharge-able cordless electric mower. A gasoline mower wouldn't be safe for him, and the odds are good that he would run over an elec-tric cord. Because Beth is his guardian, her name is also on his checking account, and while he can't keep track of the account himself, with her help he used his debit card to buy the mower. She goes on to explain that she is expected to use part of his and Coleen's small SSI checks each month to pay some rent and food. The money left in their accounts they spend under Beth's watch-ful eye. David has little number sense, so he is completely depen-dent on Beth regarding financial matters. Coleen's math is weak, and while she understands numbers and money, she still needs guidance.

When we get ready to leave the house, Beth goes to a particu-lar spot in the living room directly over Coleen's bedroom and bangs on the hardwood floor with a heavy toy. "She can hear low sounds", Beth says. When Coleen promptly comes upstairs, Beth explains that she's leaving, and that Baby Jeffrey, who will be home from supervised parent visitation in two hours, will need a bottle and a nap. Coleen makes it clear that she understands by repeating the information and goes back downstairs. Beth tells David what time he should make sure that Coleen is upstairs. He looks at his watch and nods. Coleen is responsible, but a backup system is always good!

This morning Mercedes has a round of medical appointments. The teen doesn't feel good, perhaps because her blood pressure is low, her lupus is causing problems, or maybe because she just ate one too many slices of pizza the night before. Beth coaches her before we leave the house: "To stay out of the hospital, when the doctor asks you how you are today, give her a smile when you answer." This, I think, is no nonsense medical foster care by a nurse. It's not in Mercedes's best interest to be hospitalized unless it's really necessary.

Mercedes reacts to the suggestion by rolling her eyes and grimacing, but an hour later, when the doctor asks her how she feels, Mercedes smiles and says, "Not great, but okay. I have a little stomach ache." Behind the doctor's back Beth grins and gives Mercedes a "thumbs up" sign. The good news from the nephrologist, or kidney specialist, today is that, based on the information regarding her dialysis yesterday, her blood pressure, and her weight, she can increase both her limited liquid intake and her sodium. This is great news for a teenager who is coping with an extremely limited diet.

Beth explores with the doctor the idea of a portable dialysis machine that Mercedes could use at home every night, instead of going to the hospital three times a week. The upside is that Mercedes would be able to go to the beach with the rest of the Sylvia Street gang and perhaps reenroll in school. The downside would be that Beth would have to administer the dialysis. She could never be away from Mercedes for a night, unless someone else were trained and hired to handle it. The catch? A trained person has to administer it regularly for that patient in order for it to be done safely, and that would be expensive. Just ten hours of overnight care by a medically-trained person at perhaps thirty dollars an hour would cost Beth about half of the entire month's allowance she receives for Mercedes, and there are no funds available to cover respite care. When a child lives with his or her own family, an aunt or grandmother is often trained to be a backup person for nighttime dialysis. Neither Beth nor Mercedes have that extended family member with a vested interest to be the backup person. The doctor recognizes the dilemma, and, having no solution, suggests that they keep discussing the idea, meaning at next month's appointment.

At Beth's request, the doctor examines Mercedes's gastronomy button, the place where two cans of nightly liquid nutrition are pumped directly into her stomach. Beth has noticed that Mercedes has outgrown the button, and needs a larger size. A new one is ordered, and when it arrives, Beth will take care of the procedure at home, swapping out the one that is too small. She comments that the procedure is akin to piercing an ear.

Next it's down the hall for Mercedes's physical therapy session. Beth and I visit while Mercedes works with the therapist. She catches me up on what's going on with the girl. The problems with her leg going numb have been diagnosed as conversion disorder, also known as psychosomatic seizures. She has no control over them, and they are not triggered by stress at the moment of the seizure, but they are a psychological reaction to overwhelming physical and emotional stress.

When counseling was recommended as one way to help, Mercedes asked, "Why would I need counseling?"

"Well," Beth said, "This happens because you have stress in your life that makes your brain have seizures. Your father has not been there for you, you have lupus, you're on dialysis, you aren't in school, and you've lost contact with the friends you had before you got sick. You have some things to talk about."

After several counseling appointments, paid for by the state, the seizure activity has decreased. The counselor has Mercedes reading about lupus, so she can understand and begin to accept her illness. She's also helping her to deal clearly with her father: instead of defending him and making excuses for him, maybe she can move toward recognizing his significant shortcomings as a parent and forgive him for those.

Several months ago Mercedes was adamant that she was only staying with Beth for a month or two. Now she says that the minute she turns eighteen (several years from now), she'll be gone. Also of significance, she no longer corrects people when they call Beth her mother or her foster mother.

When physical therapy is finished, Beth requests that the therapist provide documentation for all Mercedes's physical therapy hours so the school will consider giving her physical education credit. The therapist promises to email Beth the dates and hours the very next day, and we leave for the lab. That's just one small example of the advocacy role that a foster parent plays. Who else will advocate for a child in foster care? Not the biological parent. That's why the child is in foster care. Not the case worker who visits only occasionally. Not the official, who makes final decisions about placement or health directives but may never personally meet a child. The ongoing advocate for Mercedes in this case is clearly Beth.

Next it's time for a blood draw to see the status of several things: most importantly, her lupus. When the blood test is complete, Mercedes selects a treat from the gift box. While most of the gifts are toys, she finds a real harmonica which appeals to her. On the way home, Beth suggests that she go online to learn how to play it.

When we arrive back at the house, Mercedes has a seizure as she walks across the yard. When her leg goes numb, she freezes, trying to keep her balance. Beth, still in the car, calls out the window, "Stay on the grass, so if you fall, your head won't hit the sidewalk!" It seems harsh, but they both laugh. Not making a big deal out of them is part of the therapy.

Everyone has something to ask or tell Beth when we enter the house. Trina feels much better, and her blood sugar is okay. Markie repeats her information about moving on in school next year. David wants to know if Beth has line-dancing class tonight. Coleen reports on the short duration of Baby Jeffrey's nap and accentuates her frustration with an eye roll and a hand gesture that suggests *I've had it.* Jeffrey makes his one sound: "Uh-uh- uh-uh!"

Gracious as ever, or just wanting absolute clarity about chairs at the table, David asks me if I'm staying for dinner. He's clearly disappointed when I tell him no, which, I must say, makes me feel good. He wants me to stay so that I join them at their church tomorrow night for a spaghetti dinner. Their church offers free dinners to the neighborhood occasionally. On those nights, the Sylvia Street gang goes, and Beth helps cook and serve.

I tell Beth that I'm impressed by this offering to the community. She wryly says, "Yeah, last month a kid brought his whole soccer team after practice. I don't think they were short on food at their homes, but it made our numbers look good."

THE ENTRY HALL

THE FRONT DOOR opens into a large entryway next to the living room. Hundreds of kids have passed through this hall on their way to a permanent home or adult independence. Case workers have come to deliver kids into Beth's care, and then, given their overloaded schedules, too rarely crossed the sill for home visits. School district tutors have brought their lessons and their expertise to home-bound students. Police cars have brought for the night children found wandering with obvious medical needs and no family yet identified.

Hanging on the entryway wall is a collection of a dozen or more crosses from around the world. Some are metal, some straw, some porcelain, and they are both simple and ornate, both large and small. Beth collects them on her travels and has received some as gifts. No other religious art work or is displayed in the house, but the collection makes a quiet visual statement that this is a Christian household.

Baby Jeffrey likes to play with the mail slot next to the door. It's just his height, and he can make the metal flap bang. It's extra special if someone out on the porch bends down to peek into the slot or wiggles a finger inside. I know that from personal experience!

The entry hall could also be called the exit hall, and, unfortunately, the reentry hall. Only two months after Shontel and Jaytee left Sylvia Street with their sock monkeys, Beth and the caseworker flew to the Midwest to bring them back. In an email, she explains that the adoptive mom had many more kids in the home than she had told officials and displayed, they said, an alarming pattern of deception. I wonder what Shontel told her former classmates when she returned to her old school and what room she now sleeps in since Trina took her place? Did she bring her sock monkey back? How confusing is this for Jaytee? What must be going through Beth's mind? I guess she'll postpone buying new drapes.

Over several emails I get a clearer picture of children going through a really rough time. Shontel's therapist describes them as being disregulated, an emotional reaction to over-the-top stress and sense of dislocation or abandonment. This agitated state understandably results in screaming, fighting, tantrums and rages make that make these children tough to be around. The catch is, the last thing a child who feels dislocated or abandoned needs is to be ignored or sent to her room.

To help weather the storm, Alily has agreed to visit and help out for a few days. She misses Beth and the liveliness of the house on Sylvia Street. Her help is not a long term solution for Shontel, though. What is? Therapy and patience, maybe.

Beth says that Shontel doesn't want to go to school and doesn't want to go to day camp this summer, but the foster mom knows her own limits, I think. For Beth to keep her sanity, she'll need some breathing room and a chance to go out to lunch with friends or attend a dance class.

It looks like I need to arrange another visit. The thing is: no matter when I go or stop going to visit, there are kids in flux, moving out or moving in, getting better or declining in health. It's a river passing by, and whenever I dip a toe into it, the water is different. When I asked Beth what she wants me to say about her work, she says she doesn't work, that she just has a life. An intense life, I might add.

SUMMER

THE BEACH

Going to the beach in the summer has been a long-standing tradition for Beth. For many, many years, she has rented a house on the Pacific coast that is big enough for her current household and part of her biological family to spend the week together. When I ask her about joining her for a few days this summer, she is gracious and welcoming. Her email says come early, stay all week, come back to Sylvia Street afterward. She assures me that there is room in the house for me, although it may mean sleeping on a couch. While I am welcome all week, she does caution that three or four twenty-four hour days might be all I can handle. I take her advice and make a reservation at a bed and breakfast inn a few miles from her beach house for the second half of the week in the middle of August.

She explains to me that some foster kids have a terrible time with vacations. Their past histories of packing a suitcase and going someplace else have often meant something other than a fun-filled family trip. It's likely that travelling is associated with eviction or fear.

There are three things that make a vacation enjoyable, Beth explains to me: one, the anticipation; two, the actual vacation; and three, the memories. This makes sense to me; I consider a recent trip. I looked forward to visiting my son and his family across the country even before I booked my flight. I made lists and thought about what special gift I wanted to give my granddaughter. My time with my son and his family was delightful. We talked over savory

*dinners; we heard good street music and hiked in the woods. I snug-
gled with my granddaughter. I came home with photos, stories, and
great memories. It's a part of the package called a vacation.*

*From a foster parent class and experience, Beth learned that for
a child prior to entering foster care, these three aspects are not the
same. There is, perhaps, no delicious anticipation of a trip; it comes
out of the blue when a parent suddenly decides to take off with the
children in order to avoid abuse or escape creditors. Maybe the trip is
horrible with lonely nights in a motel while mom goes out to work or
party. Maybe the children never return home to school, friends, and
toys. Their memories? Maybe only bad ones. When that's been the
experience, children can build up stress as the vacation approaches
and fret about leaving most of their belongings at home, assuming
they will never see them again. When the vacation starts, if nothing
bad happens, they may make something bad happen, just to relieve
the stress.*

*Knowing this, and having experienced it in the past, Beth has
nevertheless continued to go to the beach each year. She says, "This
is what families do. They go on vacation." One year a member of the
family was a wheelchair-bound teenage girl, a tiny young woman
with few words. The beach itself was too much for her, but each
afternoon Beth laid her in a wading pool on the deck for a little
while, and the girl took great pleasure in looking out at the Pacific,
listening to the surf, and feeling the ocean breeze blow over her.*

*This year, nobody going to the beach has a traumatic history
involving motels and trips, and no one is wheelchair bound. The biggest challenge for Beth is locating a center where Mercedes can have
dialysis three times while they're away from home.*

*My anticipation is high. I pack beach clothes, bedding, sun-
screen, a couple books, my computer, and some contributions for
the kitchen. My packing list is quite short. Beth's list? Two columns
top to bottom on an eight-by-eleven piece of note book paper.*

A Summer Saturday

W HEN I ARRIVE on Sylvia Street, Beth is loading the van. I roll down my window as I pull to the curb. "Somebody here goin' on vacation?"

"Vacation, are you kidding? You've got the wrong house. This is going to be a lot of work!" She laughs.

While Coleen, Trina, Mercedes, and, to my surprise Alily and a girl I have yet to meet load the van, Shontel and Jaytee are eating lunch at the table. Shontel, who has been asking since ten o'clock, is happy to finally be eating lunch since Beth informed her that they will be leaving for the beach right after lunch. Jeffrey is eating noodles, I notice, a food he could not handle in the spring.

"Every girl between the ages of ten and twenty-four report to the laundry room and take your clean stuff!" Beth calls out. Ten minutes later she checks the laundry room. There is still some clean laundry. She repeats the call and the girls come back to collect more clothing.

Beth sits down at the table with her long packing list and crosses off the last few things: her book, salad dressing, Trina's insulin. She asks David to take out the recycling and garbage and checks the refrigerator one last time. She stuffs a few toys from the toy basket into a half-full bag, and we're off.

Maureen, Beth's forty-something biological daughter, has already left for the beach with two sons, Aden and Travis, and also

Markie. Janie, Maureen's lifelong friend, drives the eight person van with Coleen, Mercedes, Trina, and her own daughter, Aurora.

Beth drives the fourteen-person van which transports the rest of the household, plus the two young women, Alily and Nadeen, Beth's seventeen year old god daughter, invited to come along for a free beach vacation in exchange for childcare help.

David asks if he can ride with me. I agree to have him in my car, and during the trip from the city to the beach that takes several hours with weekend traffic, our conversation ebbs and flows. He asks me if I have AAA membership. When I say no, he's shocked. "What do you do if you lock your keys in the car, or if you have a dead battery or a flat tire?" I can hear in his voice his disappointment in my bad judgment.

I stretch the truth, saying, "Oh, my car insurance covers all of that!" He's relieved.

He asks me many questions about my car, and we sustain the give and take of conversation about the vehicle. When I ask him about his leg brace, though, wondering if it helps his leg not hurt when he walks or just makes it stronger, he just says "I don't know." End of discussion.

Within twenty minutes, he's sure that Beth has already arrived at the beach because we can't see her van ahead of us. Later, when we pull up to the house and she's not there yet because they've made a bathroom stop on the way, he's surprised.

Everyone helps unload the cars and vans when we arrive. There are seventeen of us, so there are lots of supplies, clothes, beach gear, and an incredible amount of groceries to carry inside. My contributions include sandwich, quart, and gallon plastic bags, garbage bags, paper towels, coffee, peanut butter, and a few boxes of cereal. Beth puts a variety of medications and supplements in a high kitchen cupboard. She gives each of her charges a large mesh bag with instructions for handling dirty laundry. It is clear that Beth needs a fair degree of order and tidiness to be comfortable. The garbage can is moved to a little table in the corner, so Jeffrey can't reach it. It seems he has taken a liking to adding things or removing things from any garbage can or waste basket within reach.

For Trina, Mercedes, and me, it's our first time at the beach house. Everyone else has been here before, most of them for summers as long as they can remember. Sitting at the dining room table and looking out the glass sliding doors past the deck to the ocean directly in front of us, Mercedes says softly, "I could live here all the time." It's possible she's never seen the ocean.

"Me too, even when it is stormy."

"Oh, that might be scary." she responds.

"There's scary, and then there's scary. I know wind and crashing waves can't hurt me when I'm in a cozy beach house. Different kinds of things, not weather, scare me." I tell her.

She considered this for a moment. "Well, I guess it's kind of the same for me. Maybe."

While we gaze at the ocean, Maureen, Janie and their children check out the beach with Jaytee and Shontel. Then David asks me to help him find TV stations on the bedroom set. He has been randomly pushing buttons on two remotes for several minutes. Eventually I find the right combination for the satellite dish receiver and the television. He sits very close to the set to watch, and I am reminded that even with strong glasses, his eyesight is weak.

WHILE BETH PREPARES spaghetti with warm garlic bread and a green salad for dinner, I unbox and assemble the new booster chair with a food tray that will work as a highchair for Jeffrey when strapped to a dining chair. When dinner is ready we gather for grace. It's an informal buffet, unlike dinner on Sylvia Street. Some eat outside on the deck, some on high stools at the counter, and some enjoy their food at the dining table. In addition to Mercedes's restricted diet, Trina's diabetes-related issues, and Jeffrey's eating difficulties, Aden and Travis have non-health related, but fairly dramatic, food issues regarding texture and flavor, evidenced by just plain spaghetti noodles on their plates. No salad. No garlic bread.

After dinner, Beth announces that the girls, starting with the oldest, will each take a night doing dishes. Nobody complains or questions the decision. Fortunately, there's a large dishwasher, and everybody except Jaytee has scraped and stacked their own plates. Coleen, the oldest, gets right to work. David performs his usual job: garbage removal, but he's frustrated because this beach community doesn't have a recycling program. Seeing a pop can in the garbage momentarily confuses him, and upsets him even when the lack of recycling facilities is explained to him.

While cleanup is in process, Janie brings out a big batch of chocolate chip cookie dough she prepared at home and bakes three sheets of cookies so everybody gets a warm dessert.

Having discovered the cleaning closet, Jaytee, Shontel, and Jeffrey decide to use the broom, the dust mop, and the carpet sweeper. With persistence and diligence, if not efficiency or effectiveness, they work on the floors and carpet. Amazingly, no teen or adult is poked in the face, and no glass is knocked off the table by an errant mop or broom handle.

David wants the large flat screen TV in the living room to work, so he randomly pushes buttons on two remotes again for some time before asking for help. This time Janie comes to his rescue. He wants to watch infomercials, but Beth discourages him, and he switches to a cartoon show. After a few minutes he loses interest and starts picking up the poker chips that Jeffrey has found and scattered across the rug. It will become a repeated activity throughout the week: Jeffrey scatters and David collects. For Jeffrey, it's pure delight. For David it seems to be a combination of pleasure and frustration. Maybe that's the definition of an obsession.

After dessert, the teenagers go downstairs to read, watch movies on their computers, or talk on their cell phones. Aden and Travis speak with their dad, who's back home on the eastern side of the state, and play a video game with Aurora.

The little ones go off to bed, and it's now just adults in the living room. We talk for a while before heading to bed ourselves.

"Should we try and go to the county fair one day? It's going on all week." Maureen asks.

"Even with kid prices, it'll cost a lot of money for this group." Janie offers.

"It would have to be Tuesday or Thursday, because Monday and Wednesday Mercedes has dialysis and Friday is Shontel's birthday. But Janie's right. It's expensive. Maybe we ride the train one day instead. And I'm thinking we all go to Astoria on Wednesday. Take lunch and spend the day." Beth says.

"Maybe see if the weather's good for being on the beach Tuesday before we decide on fair or train, huh?" Janie says, and the others take that as the closing statement for the discussion. Nothing is definitive, but everybody's comfortable.

I can feel the casualness of vacation in their talk. In fact, the relaxed dinner routine and the easy way that the old, young, and very young have become one household, taking care of chores and playing together, make it clear that the beach house is a different world.

After promising to start coffee in the morning before taking a jog on the beach, Maureen and Janie head to bed.

"I won't be jogging." Beth announces. "Goodnight."

I roll out my bedding on the couch and read for a while before turning off the lamp.

In the middle of the night, Coleen drags her bedding upstairs and settles on another couch. Curiously, she complains about the noise from the other girls. She is, after all, almost deaf and wears earplugs and an eye mask.

THE BEACH HOUSE

WE STAY IN a large and simply furnished beach house located just back from the beach. The lower floor has a garage with a ping pong table where Markie sleeps in a tent with the dog. There is also a big family room with a sofa bed, a double/twin bunk, and a futon. Trina, Mercedes, Coleen, Nadine, and Alily sleep there. Maureen and her two sons share a downstairs bedroom; Janie and her daughter Aurora sleep on big air mattresses in the downstairs kitchen, which for our group is only used to store food and the ever-present laundry. At the top of the stairs, the door opens into a large living room with three comfortable couches and a flat screen TV. The dining table seats six, and there are four swivel stools at a long counter facing the well-stocked kitchen. Beth, Baby Jeffrey, and Shontel share one bedroom, while David and Jaytee share the other. Both Shontel and Jaytee have made nests for themselves by putting their air mattresses and sleeping bags in the bedroom closets. Fortunately, there are bathrooms both upstairs and downstairs.

Floor-to-ceiling windows and a glass sliding door provide a panoramic view of the Pacific. The sliding door opens onto a deck running the width of the house with two tables and several chaise lounges. Nothing but a row of shrubs is between the front yard and the beach. Jaytee notices when a small fishing boat passes by. When he first arrived, he kept asking about the noise. "Ocean waves?"

he'd repeat when someone would answer him. The other sound he cares about is the train carrying tourists from one beach town to the next and back three or four times a day. It blows its whistle near the house, since the road to our driveway crosses the tracks.

A Summer Sunday

THE DAY BEGINS with Janie's Belgium waffles from two irons and coffee, whose simultaneous preparation results in a blown fuse. Maureen is on it immediately. Keeping the coffee maker going is paramount; making waffles two at a time is almost as important for a household of seventeen, so she uses outlets on different circuits.

After they get out of bed, Shontel and Jaytee each spend a few minutes snuggling on Beth's lap.

"How did you sleep?" I ask Shontel.

"I watched a lot of TV." I'm surprised, but then she explains. "I have a TV computer in my head and watch during the night."

Beth adds that once in a while Shontel will tell her. "I watched a good movie last night when I was asleep, Mom. No monsters." What a great way for a six year old to describe dreaming!

Baby Jeffrey spends a few minutes in Beth's lap taking part of a bottle and waking up, and then zooms nonstop around the room, trying to climb on everything, including Coleen. He pulls her hair and her blankets. Jeffrey's the only one who can wake her up without her growling and snapping. Jeffrey has added a few sounds to his vocabulary. bah! as well as gah gah!, and uh! uh! Rarely but clearly, he says Mama. At this point, he's using most of his sounds to wake Coleen.

By late morning, everyone is up. Jaytee is busy using a carpet sweeper on every part of the floor. Shontel has found the poker chips in the end table and is distributing them.

When I ask her why I get poker chips, she explains. "These are church vitamins. I'm the pastor. I have blueberry vitamins and vanilla vitamins. The red chips are the grape juice, and that they have fluoride in them." No other adult who's taking the poker chips she's handing them as they converse seem to know that they're part of Shontel's version of Sunday morning communion with fluoride thrown in for good measure.

Janie and Maureen's kid have gone downstairs to play. The teenage girls shower, do their hair, talk on their cell phones, and watch videos, except for Mercedes curls up on the couch and reads.

Eventually, with a bit of planning and discussion about who will supervise, most people head for the beach. Little kids wear sunblock and neoprene jackets or vests that will keep them warm; Maureen and Janie have wet suits for themselves, their own children, and Nadine. Alily, who lived as a child in the South Pacific, doesn't want to swim in the cold water, but she goes to the beach to help with the children. Markie and Coleen don't like the wind and the sand and it's difficult for David to navigate the sand and logs, so those three stay in the house with Beth and the baby. Trina is willing to walk to the beach, but not go in the water. Though her stamina is limited, Mercedes wants to join the group. She dresses warmly and, bless her heart, walks down with us. I carry a big bag of sand toys down for Jaytee and Shontel.

Once on the beach, some body surf while others sit on logs and talk to each other or on cell phones. Nadine plays in the sand with Jaytee. Shontel asks for my help in making a sign with a flat piece of driftwood and a piece of charcoal. She wants it to say "Driftwood Beach". She's frustrated when we can't make it stand up like a real sign. Eventually I give up. Maureen, now out of the water, comes over and tries to solve the problem. Shontel moves on to another sand and driftwood project. After a time Maureen gives up, too.

I park myself on a log and talk with Trina for a while.

"Think how different this beach view would be without those giant rock monoliths out in the water." I say.

"Everything is like that. Change one thing, and everything changes." She tells me.

Trina is smart, and mature for her years and probably worldly in ways I don't want to know about. She's artsy and fashionable in a bumbling fourteen-year-old way. She's also interested in Buddhism. Maybe she's an old soul, as they say, but at the same time she's very naïve, and ignorant about some really basic life skills. Plus, Beth reminded me earlier in the year, Trina is very complicated and has deep emotionally wounds, in part, from parental neglect. She would willingly continue our discussion, but I decide that I need exercise in this brisk air, so I take a walk and she returns to conversation with Alily. Exhausted by the elements and the four-minute walk to beach, Mercedes has gone back to the house.

After my walk, I take paint brushes, water color pencils, and paper to the deck I like to dabble in paint while vacationing, and intentionally brought extra supplies. Markie, Aurora, and Nadine, who I learn is a skilled artist, join me.

While we paint, Markie talks. She tells me about her dog, how she got her, and how important animals are to her. "Animals feed my spirit", she says, "The way kids and babies feed Mama's spirit."

She speaks like a teenager yet paints like a seven-year-old. Her paper includes a blue wavy ocean and a triangle of yellow sun shining from the top right corner, even though it's a gray day with light clouds and no distinct sun. Markie also talks about where she'd like to live as an adult. She doesn't want to live alone, and she recognizes that she needs to live where she can get some support.

"I'm not so good with things like money," she says. "But the trouble is, I don't want this to sound bad, but I'm not like a lot of other people with special needs. Some of those people drive me crazy."

She's right about that. Markie's a complicated person. She's reads at a first-grade level, but on her phone are two artistic photos of beautiful insects she noticed while waiting for the school bus. She can't always follow people's conversations, and her conversations with others usually consist of her talking and the other person listening; that's what's happening here at the painting table here on the deck. And yet, as is also true right now, she has a degree of self-awareness that is surprising.

While Markie continues talking, Nadine works quietly creating a stunning seascape. She knows how to use watercolors to make a cloudy sky. She sprinkles table salt on the wet paper and in a few minutes: mottled clouds! Her painting is a beautiful and accurate representation of the beach in front of us except for the added ruby-colored beach umbrella and several seabirds.

When everyone is back from the beach and showered or maybe just de-sanded, dinner, prepared by Beth, is almost ready. It's a taco salad bar meal tonight, and when everyone is assembled, we say and sign grace and then eat. Maureen's kids can't deal with salad or with taco meat, so they eat chips with cheese or peanut butter sandwiches. Janie pulls out the cookie dough and bakes just enough cookies for everyone to have one or two.

Janie then brings out her daughter's easel and some of us take part in an informal game using the cards from a Pictionary deck, and people take turns drawing a word and having people guess what it is. Coleen can't play because she can't hear the guesses people are throwing out. Trina and Alily half-heartedly play and Mercedes sits among us reading another title in a vampire series she's enjoying. Maureen and Janie keep all the elementary-aged kids actively involved in the game. Eventually, David wants a turn. What does he draw? A vacuum cleaner. There is a moment of awed silence in the room, when he writes the "vacuum" under his drawing. Considering he can't read, we are shocked and shower him with praise. He's so overwhelmed by the attention that he leaves the room to watch TV in the bedroom.

Baby Jeffrey and Jaytee play underfoot until they practically drop in their tracks. Alily helps Jaytee into his pajamas, brushes his teeth, and puts him to bed. Beth fixes a bottle for Jeffrey. After Coleen has given it to him, he's off to bed. Nadine helps Shontel with her bedtime routine.

With the little ones asleep, the cards come out. First Beth and Nadine play a game for two. I join them and we switch to gin rummy. Travis and Markie join in, and we play several boisterous rounds of 'spoons'. It's a card game akin to musical chairs where there is one fewer spoon on the table than there are players. In order to get a spoon, one must collect four of a kind as cards are passed around. Markie can pass the cards, but she is never able to get four of a kind; the strategy of keeping and discarding cards is beyond her, despite Beth's attempts to help her. I'm new to the game, so I get excited whenever I get four of a kind. Beth gently points out that being quiet and subtle when I match four cards and stealthily taking a spoon makes the spoon grabbing more interesting. So Markie and I both work at it. She tries to understand how to collect the right cards, and I work on subtlety. Both of us struggle!

Just as we decide to end the lively game, Nadine's mother arrives to pick her up. It's the end of a month-long stay with Beth, and the hugs and sad faces show me that this departure is hard for everyone. The Sylvia Street family loves Nadine, and she loves them. More than once Beth had told me how the value of her cheerful help with the little ones in the summer routine far outweighed the burden of another teenager in the house. She also shared that since Nadine will be starting her senior year in the fall, and has planned a trip to Europe next July and August before starting college, this might be the end of the long summer visits that have been happening for six or seven years.

People are quiet after Nadine leaves, and head off to bed. I notice that the little knob to turn off the lamp next to the couch is missing. I check the floor, the crevices between the couch cushions, and the garbage. Nothing. Jaytee has been busy.

A Summer Monday

At eight o'clock the household begins to stir. Beth drinks her first Diet Pepsi of the day and gives Jeffrey a bottle. Shontel and Jaytee slowly wander out. While the summer has been a difficult one for them, the relaxed vacation schedule is a blessing for this troubled twosome. There are no demands to finish breakfast in a timely manner, no expectations to be dressed quickly. At day camp throughout July, Jaytee required a one-on-one aide to monitor him. Shontel's behavior at day camp had also been inappropriate at times, with hitting and spitting. Here at the beach, they are just vacation kids, and their issues are not obvious.

By eight-thirty, Mercedes is dressed and ready to head to Astoria for dialysis. Maureen and Janie are taking everyone else blueberry picking. Before we leave, Beth clarifies who will be in charge of the little ones. Alily will be responsible for Shontel and Jaytee, and Coleen will take care of Jeffery. Maureen will make sure that Trina checks her blood sugar.

Beth, Mercedes and I leave in the smaller van. It takes almost an hour to get to Astoria, a town at the mouth of the Columbia River where Oregon and Washington meet. It's the closest location for pediatric dialysis. The narrow two-lane coastal highway is full of summer travelers, trucks, and long distance bicycle riders. While it's not a fast trip, it is very scenic route, passing through small towns, coastal forests, and fresh seafood vendors with crude hand-painted signs. The travel time gives Beth and me the opportunity to trade reading recommendations, and she tells me stories about other summers at the beach.

I mention Alily. "It seems like she's enjoying the opportunity to be with the family for the week, both the little ones and the teens."

"She lives a pretty sheltered life with her parents, and doesn't get to spend much time with other young people or with other English speakers, for that matter."

Then, as the highway turns a sharp corner, so does the conversation. She mentions that the younger sister is showing signs of the same immune disorder that almost killed Alily and required, eventually, a bone marrow transplant.

"You know, she says, the disorder that was caused by her family's exposure to the long lasting effects of nuclear testing when her family lived in the South Pacific."

"What? Tell me about this!"

"I don't have much information. You know, HIPAA rules, or maybe it's, I don't know." She doesn't finish her thought. HIPAA is the federal rule protecting the privacy of a patient's health information. I'm puzzled. *Not sharing information with the medical foster mom?* For a few minutes I'm speechless. I try to make sense of this information without erupting in anger. As we near Astoria, I make a mental note to learn something about atomic testing in the South Pacific when I get home.

ASTORIA IS AN old town by West Coast standards; the oldest American settlement west of the Rockies, it began as Fort Astoria, a fur-trading fort built by John Jacob Astor in 1810. Eventually the lumber and fishing industries transformed the settlement into an important town on the northwest coast. Today about ten thousand people depend a great deal on tourism. Victorian houses on its steep hillsides, red brick buildings, and businesses with Finnish or other Scandinavian names give hints of its vibrant past. When we drive past a book store in one of the large old structures on Main Street which at one time operated as a bank, both Beth and Mercedes take note. "Maybe we can stop this afternoon." Beth comments.

The more modern and relatively sleek medical complex where the dialysis center is located sits in direct contrast to the vintage look of the town itself. The waiting room has signs suggesting that Mercedes is not the only vacationer using this place. This center, it turns out, is part of a business placing dialysis centers across the country in vacation locales. When we check in, the other patients all seem to be elderly with assorted medical issues. The nurse wisely gives Mercedes a place at the end of the room, at considerable distance from the old men receiving dialysis.

When Mercedes is situated, Beth and I leave to meet up with a friend from nursing school who has retired to the area. We join her for a leisurely lunch at a seafood restaurant, and she and Beth catch up on each other's lives: new grandchildren, health issues of elderly parents, highlights of the last year, and plans for the coming year. It's a friendship that easily picks up where it left off. She drives us around the area, giving us ideas for activities when we return with the whole household for the day.

Mercedes is not quite done when we return to the medical center, so while we wait, Beth and I talk, and I hear about the free three-day kidney family camp.

"We all went except for Coleen and David. They stayed home. The rest of us stayed in a cabin and I had day care for the little ones. Well," she says, rolling her eyes, "except for Jaytee, who was asked not to come back the second day because of his misbehavior." She describes classes and workshops for parents, and support groups, as well as activities and classes for Mercedes and the other kids with kidney issues. I am struck by the value of getting teens with end-stage renal disease or new kidney transplants together to talk, to learn from other, to be with people who understand a little bit about their lives. Listening to Beth, I get the sense that most kids are either waiting for a new kidney or adjusting to a new kidney. Mercedes is in neither position, I think, because of her lupus.

Turns out I'm wrong. Her medical team now believes that once they get her lupus under control, a transplant is perhaps possible. That's a ways off in the future, however. Right now in addition to everything else, she's not producing platelets in her blood.

When we leave the center, Mercedes reports with pleasure that she had spent the time on a heated bed that kept her warm during the procedure. A small pleasure, I know, but her gratitude is evident.

We do stop at the bookstore. Mercedes finds a thick paperback she wants. Beth buys an easy reader for Shontel about Amber Brown, a popular children's book character, going into second grade. Shontel has expressed fears about second grade. She had the same caring teacher for kindergarten and first grade, except for the difficult time in the Midwest, so moving up means a new classroom and a new teacher. Beth and I pass by a display of best-selling mystery and crime novels. "Ah, some old friends," she says, touching the covers of books she has read.

"Doesn't the gore bother you?" I ask. She explains that skimming past the really gory parts doesn't weaken the novel for her because it's the solving of the crime and the psychology of the criminals and the detectives that she finds most interesting.

"I hope that Maureen and Janie have planned for the hot dog roast on the beach tonight, because if I have to start dinner when we get back to the house, it's gonna' be a late dinner!" Beth comments when we're about twenty minutes away. We don't call to find out. We just hope.

It turns out that Maureen is just as smart and capable as her mother, and has made a decision based on logistics and weather.

When we arrive at the beach house, we can see the smoke of the fire Maureen and Janie have started on the beach.

David has waited for us to come home, but now, using his crutches, slowly makes his way across the logs. It's his only trip to the beach all week, but it's an important one. This is the hot dog roast, and more importantly, the s'mores dessert. Mercedes and I find sweatshirts and walk down. Beth grabs her camera and a Diet Pepsi.

A few minutes later, sitting on a log watching this disparate crew, I'm momentarily overcome by the wonderful ordinariness of this vacation moment. Beth is snapping photos. "This is what families do," she says. "They take photos on their summer vacations." She makes sure she captures everybody in at least one picture.

David is momentarily stymied when someone else joins me on the log, so that he can't sit next to me to eat his hot dog. Markie holds her hot dog in the flames. Trina finds the best part of the fire for roasting her hot dog: no flames, just a red and glowing bowl of heat on one side of the fire. She carefully turns her stick again and again. Jaytee fences with his stick until it's grabbed out of his hand. Baby Jeffrey toddles over to a piece of driftwood and throws up whatever he had eaten. Janie tosses the driftwood down the beach, and kicks sand over what's left of his indigestion problem so we don't have to look at it. Mercedes roasts a second hot dog. Beth notices, and frowns, but doesn't say anything. I wonder if it will make Mercedes sick.

Markie and Shontel are ready for s'mores before anyone else. A sweet and gooey assembly line begins as people roast, char, or barely heat their marshmallows and take them to Beth to be sandwiched with a piece of chocolate inside graham crackers. Sticky fingers and faces provide more photo opportunities.

The teenagers, caught up in the fascination of glowing embers that is eternally human, stand around the dying fire. No one is texting or listening to music. It's just the beach at sunset with a slight breeze and people gathered around a fire.

When the fire is dead, we scatter the ashes, and pack up. Everyone, except the baby and David, helps carry food, garbage, chairs, and toys back to the house. The little ones are exhausted. Alily gives Shontel and Jaytee quick baths. Beth washes Jeffrey and fixes him a bottle. Within the hour, the little ones are asleep. Maureen's boys talk with their dad on the phone and play a video game with Aurora. Others watch TV, use their phones, or read. Trina and Beth have a conversation about how the girl handled her blood sugar levels today. I don't catch the details, but I can tell that it has not been Trina's best self-monitoring day. Mercedes's second hot dog was a mistake. In the last hour and a half, she has thrown up twice. Beth sighs. She could have called out to Mercedes at the fire, "No, stop!" but this was probably the girl's first ever beach fire and hot dog roast, so she didn't, she tells me.

Shortly after I turn in on a couch, Coleen settles into another couch with her earplugs and eye mask. No one seems to understand why she needs to do this, but whatever works, right?

A Summer Tuesday

When Jaytee walks into the living room in the morning, he announces, "I'm here!" It isn't a triumphal comment. It's just a cheerful fact, and it helps me start the day on a good note. We all gradually wake-up and eat breakfast. The teenagers, of course, are last to join us. Maureen and Janie have been up for hours, jogging on the beach. Alily helps the little ones dress, and I see that they are both in their summer library program T-shirts, another reason to smile.

It's going to be a beach day, so Maureen and Janie make plans for which kids and teens will join them. Beth makes sure that Jaytee and Shontel have specific supervisors. She takes responsibility for Jeffrey. A summer vacation at the beach unfolds, and it would be hard to tell, looking at this group, who needs a one-on-one aide at summer day camp, who needs counseling, who needs weekly medical appointments, and who has major disabilities. After a lunch break, the baby naps, some return to the beach, some read, and David sits on a deck swing and quietly sings what he's thinking. Some of what he sings might be about me, although only the ocean can hear him. His wanting to sit near me at meals and the moony look in his eyes when he gazes at me have me wondering if he's taken a special liking to me. *I'm just being silly.* I tell myself.

Midafternoon, Beth takes the baby and all the young children for a train ride back and forth from the nearest town to the next.

Before checking in at the bed and breakfast where I'll be staying the next three nights, I wait by my car in the driveway so I can wave when the train passes by. I wave madly when I see Beth, sitting with Jeffrey on her lap in an open car with the rest her group. I'm not sure any of the kids see me or understand that they have ridden past our driveway.

After checking into quietest bed and breakfast one could imagine, I head back to join the group for dinner, and since there is plenty of help in the kitchen, I offer to read with Shontel. Alternating reading to each other, we get two thirds of the way through her new book before it's time to eat. Over a meal of hamburgers and veggie burgers, I ask Jaytee and Shontel about their train ride.

Jaytee offers, "Choo, choo! All aboard!" He can't offer much other information, but it's very clear that he loved the excursion.

"We got ice cream cones before getting back on the train." Shontel reports.

Beth adds, "The ice cream vendor asked if I was a foster mom. I said 'yes,' but I don't understand why I couldn't have been seen as the grandmother of the six children I had in tow."

Later in the evening, several people choose snacks - granola bars, cheese and crackers, fruit leather - from the assortment stacked on top of the microwave. Markie pours herself a large bowlful of trail mix, and proceeds to sort out and throw away all the parts she doesn't like. Beth notices and is clearly irritated.

"What are you doing? she scolds. "Look how much you took and look how much you are throwing away. That is so wasteful!"

The girl is more confused than apologetic, and responds, "But I'm hungry! Should I be eating something else?"

Jaytee spends the entire evening driving a train, using the cold wood stove in the living room as his engine. I realize this is new. Jaytee has developed independent creative play. He's reliving the afternoon and imagining himself the engineer. As opposed to yesterday, when the missing lamp switch disturbed me, today began and now ends with good feelings about Jaytee.

THE BED AND BREAKFAST

I LET MYSELF *into the inn with an old-fashioned key and climb the wide dark wood stairway to the second floor. This inn was originally built almost ninety years ago as a bordello, catering, I assume, to the fishermen and loggers. Perhaps this explains the little parlors in several places along the hall. Since the twenties the place has been soundproofed, and it's very quiet. You can't hear traffic passing by on Highway 101.*

Before settling in for the night, I pop a bag of complimentary microwave popcorn and brew a cup of tea. My room is small, but tastefully and beautifully decorated. I arrange myself on the bed with my tea and popcorn, open up my laptop, and start looking for information on nuclear testing in the South Pacific. I get a dizzying array of hits, none of which tell me exactly what I want to know but, at the same time, tell me more than I ever want to know.

I start with Wikipedia to get terminology and a quick overview. I learn from my web searches over the next hour that after World War II the United States took responsibility for a large group of islands in the South Pacific. "Took responsibility" is a deceptive term - maybe "took control over" would be more accurate. Officially it was a Trust Authority. Given what I am learning, I think about how inappropriate the word "trust" is in this context.

The Atomic Energy Commission created what was called the Pacific Proving Grounds in 1947, and with the Department of Defense, conducted over sixty-six underwater and atmospheric atomic and hydrogen bomb tests over the course of more than a decade. American testing there ended with the signing of the Partial Test Ban Treaty in 1963, but the French, who also had territorial control in the area, continued nuclear testing into the seventies.

U.S. Department of Energy websites provide statistics about dates and tests as well as some information about health and safety issues in the Marshall Islands. From the Atlantic I get photographs. On an activist website I get tough-to-read details about whole atolls being vaporized. I learn about decommissioned ships anchored at a testing site that were so "hot" they had to be sunk. I read about radiation sickness of islanders who were assumed, before testing, to be out of danger. I read about horrific birth defects.

Given our current understanding of the possible long-term impacts of the tests, I am sickened by the ignorance or wanton disregard for life. Moreover, I'm frustrated that I can't find anything that speaks to the challenges Alily and her sisters face. They weren't alive during the testing years, nor was their mother. Are their challenges related to the food chain or to the soil? Genetics? My research produces more questions than answers. Worn out, I decide to call it a night.

A Summer Wednesday

Wednesday morning I start the day with a long soak in the deep claw-footed bathtub. When I arrive in the breakfast room, two other families are eating. I chat briefly with a couple from Galveston, Texas about their famous flood, part of what was called Isaac's Storm, which I'd read about, and when another guest joins us, we discuss touring haunted places. It seems there is talk that our inn has permanent non-paying residents! The others leave, and I use the binoculars at my window table to observe the small herd of elk grazing across the road. After a peaceful breakfast of good coffee, fresh raspberries and a toaster biscuit on vintage china, I step out into the summer morning and wait for the van to arrive.

Soon Beth is there, with David, Shontel, and Mercedes. The others are behind us in the larger van. We rendezvous at the Columbia River Maritime Museum on the waterfront in Astoria just blocks from the medical center. The plan is to check out the museum and the waterfront while Beth gets Mercedes settled in for dialysis. Jaytee wears a fuzzy teddy bear harness that looks like a small backpack with a leash. Smiling, he hands me the leash. I think the harness actually gives him a sense of security, a physical assurance in some way.

The museum is an eye-catching building with a big swoop of glass suggesting a thirty-foot wave, common in the stormy north Pacific just off the mouth of the Columbia River. The waterfront draws the group, so we head to the docks to get a closer look at the boats tied up here. Jeffrey is in a stroller, and Jaytee is on a leash, and everyone else respects the handrails on the dock, so all is good. It's a glorious sunny morning, and the breeze has the maritime pennants and flags flapping above us.

After speaking with the attendant at the museum, we decide to forego a visit: it would cost over one hundred dollars for all of us to go in, and although there are some interactive and "touchable" parts to the museum, it's not interactive enough for our particular group. A man just going into the museum grumbles that it looks like our group should have gotten a discount, but Maureen cheerfully responds, "It's okay; we want to be out in the sunshine." We tour the outside of the building, which with floor to ceiling windows gives us views of the displays, including a tug boat and a Coast Guard rescue boat responding to an emergency off the Columbia River Bar. Had I been alone, I would have gone inside. The Coast Guard's dangerous rescue work in the area nicknamed the Graveyard of the Pacific is well known. However, this trip is not about my fascination with brave sailors, but rather this cheerful and atypical family.

Before long Beth rejoins us, and we all head up the hill to visit the Astoria Column and have a picnic lunch. One of the odder tourist attractions in the area, the 1926 Astoria Column is just that: a cement column 125 feet high, patterned after Tragan's Column in Rome. The outside of the column is decorated with a wrap-around mural of the history of the area, up through the coming of the railroad in the 1880's. The inside contains a spiral staircase of 164 steps leading to an observation deck. Before any of us attempt to climb the tower, we take a lunch break. Everyone old enough to do so has packed his or her own lunch, which Maureen now pulls from an ice chest. Beth wheels over a carry-on size suitcase and unzips it. The bag is full of crackers, granola bars, corn nuts, and fruit leather to accompany the sandwiches, fruit, and yogurt people are eating.

While the group finishes lunch, Janie goes to the gift shop and buys sixteen toy balsa gliders. Almost everyone climbs to the top after lunch and sends a glider sailing into the air. Beth opts out, staying at ground level with little Jeffrey. Her grandson Travis doesn't like the claustrophobic feel of the stairway and instead collects gliders scattered on in the grass.

From the top, the view is glorious. To the east are the Cascade Mountains, and to the north the Columbia River winds its way out to the Pacific. To the west is the ocean. I'm torn between watching little gliders sail and circle down and the beauty spread out below us. Boats and barges, tiny from here, slowly move up and down the river. The infamous Columbia River Bar at the ocean's edge looks calm and innocent today.

The next stop on our excursion is the Lewis and Clark National Historic Park, a reconstruction of Fort Clatsop, the winter encampment of Lewis and Clark in 1805-06. When we enter the visitor center to pay our admission, the man at the counter asks if David has a disability pass, a free lifelong pass to National Parks. He doesn't, so Beth proceeds to sign him up for one.

"Does he have any proof on him that he is disabled?" the man asks.

No one answers. We just stare at him in disbelief. Are not leg graces, crutches, and bottle-bottom glasses visible proof? Suddenly feeling awkward, the man drops the issue and completes the paperwork for the pass.

We head out into the woods of the park and pass a life-size statue of Sacajawea and her baby next to the trail.

"Have you ever heard of Sacajawea?" I ask Alily. When she shakes her head, I explain why she is the first person we see on the trail. "She was the guide for Lewis and Clark who explored this place two hundred years ago. She was the one who knew the way and led them. And she had her baby with her!"

Alily looks with admiration at the petite statue. They are the same height.

After watching a park volunteer demonstrate how to load and shoot a musket, we walk through the reconstructed quarters. I try to imagine spending a rainy winter in these small dark spaces. We feel the soft elk skin used to make clothing. Several of us try our hand at writing with a goose feather quill pen. The volunteer demonstrates using a "pen knife" to cut the end of a feather shaft to a pen point. Trina is actually quite skilled and makes a lovely design on her sheet of paper. I awkwardly scratch out the words Fort Clatsop and marvel at the volume of words in the diaries written with these feather pens by the Corps of Discovery. We walk to the area used for cooking and eating which features a large fire pit and a log tripod. A chain with a hook for holding a large kettle over the fire is hanging from the tripod, and there are cooking utensils arranged close by. Kindling and firewood are stacked as if a fire is just about to be lit. The display, which is surrounded by a chain to keep out visitors, interests Jaytee, and he tries to climb into it. When he is told no, he erupts and tries to upend all of the stanchions holding the chain. The boy suddenly becomes an almost uncontrollable ball of fury. Thank goodness the harness keeps him from destroying the display. I see now why he might need a one-on-one aide at school or day camp. Alily, who has been holding the harness this whole time, rubs his back and talks quietly to him.

Once Jaytee calms down, several people in our group walk the broad trail down to the water where boats would have been kept. I keep thinking about the hard work of walking around in this thick underbrush before the men cleared trails. Jaytee is tired, even with smooth trails, so Trina gives him a ride on her back.

Eventually, we all meet back in the visitor center and spend time browsing in the gift shop. Beth buys Jaytee and Shontel stuffed animals – a beaver and a raccoon. She also buys a stuffed animal for Mercedes, who has not been with us today. I covet an expensive engraved bracelet with a quote from Thomas Jefferson, who sent Lewis and Clark west. "I cannot live without books," it says. I point out the bracelet to Janie, and bemoan the price. Maureen makes a quick trip to the car for a snack for Trina. Her blood sugar has gone awry, and she needs something in her system quickly.

Soon it is time for Beth, David and I to pick up Mercedes. The rest move on to Fort Stevens, a state park on the northwest tip of Oregon that had originally been part of a three-fort defense system designed to guard the entrance to the Columbia. Now, the concrete batteries built into the beach hillsides for gun emplacements are great places for kids of all ages to run around. Maureen and Janie help the kids explore the area. Then they head back to the beach house, stopping to pick up fresh crab for crab cakes on the way.

Our van stops twice on the way home, once to get Mercedes a bite to eat, and once at a large candy store in a tourist community. David wants to buy a little bit of candy for himself and some fudge for the women he sees every Monday when he vacuums the church. He's been talking about buying the women fudge all week. I realize today that he does this each year. It's a tradition, but it's not any easier for him than it was last year or the year before. Beth hands me money and asks me to accompany him to the store. He's somewhat overwhelmed by the fudge choices, and needs me to do the talking. We buy a pound of regular chocolate fudge, no nuts, and he picks out a bag of colorful candy balls for himself. When he gets back to the house, I suggest that he put away the fudge in his duffle bag so Jaytee won't see it. "Good idea," he says. They drop me at my bed and breakfast and head for the beach house.

When I drive over to join them for dinner, Janie has her laptop open on the kitchen counter, a recipe for crab cakes on the screen. I help make a salad, and we reheat pasta from an earlier meal. The crab cakes are a hit. I quietly reimburse Janie for half of the crab.

Both during and after the meal, Jeffrey seems overtired, over stimulated, or something. He vocalizes, "Eee, eee, eee" in a steady stream. When he's frustrated, it's strident, and when he's not, it's a calmer yet continuous sound. Before dinner, "Eee, eee, eee," means, *I'm hungry*. During dinner, it means *this is good* or *I want more* or *I'm done*. After dinner, "Eee, eee, eee," means I'*m playing*. It's unending. I wonder if he's been in a car seat or a stroller too much today, but I'm not the expert here. I just know that I'm tired of "eee, eee, eee." Because of that constant sound, I consider leaving right away for my quiet bed and breakfast room, but fortunately, I don't.

After the little ones are in bed, a little earlier than usual because of the long day, and the teens have moved into internet and electronic land, the adults talk in the living room. Markie, who at times like this doesn't exactly know what to do, other than eat, wisely gets out markers and paper and a tattered art book. She curls up on a sofa and tries to make copies of the pictures she likes. Maureen talks about wanting to start a "bucket list" of things that she wants to accomplish.

I mention my yearly list of new things. "I have this little blank book, and in it, I write down new foods I try, new friends I meet, new places I visit, new words I learn, and new books I read. The list needs to total my age, so each year it needs to be longer. I mean, this year it needs to be sixty-five things, and next year, sixty-six."

Beth says, "I just move from one book to another. It doesn't feel like something new, like meeting a new friend." I refrain from reminding her that she called books she has read "old friends" when we were in the book store.

"My lists wouldn't have many books on it." Maureen adds.

The conversation shifts, and Maureen turns and asks her mom when she is going to retire. I already know that Maureen, in the event of her mother's death, will sell her own house and her mother's house and buy a duplex where Coleen and David can live in one side, and she and her family can live in the other. I think Maureen is a rock star. She's busy running a business, raising two boys, tending a marriage, and cares about her vulnerable brother and sister. It's clear that she feels more responsibility than her two biological brothers.

Tonight, Maureen asks her mother for more information: "When will you retire? Who will take care of details if you become incompetent?"

"I will probably keep working until Mercedes is eighteen, if Mercedes lives that long." Beth responds. I take a deep breath. That means two things to me: Mercedes's health is really fragile, and Beth will be sixty-eight when she retires. "I worked for a hospital long enough to qualify for social security. I've been talking to a retirement expert, and I will be able to support myself in retirement." Maureen's face shows both relief and respect for her mother.

Beth's been prudent, and has been making investments for years, but she makes a point of saying, "It's difficult it is to be a full-time foster mom with no social security credit and no retirement benefits."

Maureen takes all of this in. She thinks about her own financial future. "As a small business owner, I don't have an automatic retirement plan. I'm wondering if I should myself talk with a financial planner." She returns to thinking about Beth's situation: "Should I have the contact information for the planner you've been working with?"

"I'll get that to you. She already has your and your brothers' numbers," Beth responds.

I'm as impressed by Maureen as I am by Beth. I make my farewells and leave for my inn, my mind a swirl. I have much less energy tonight than I did last night and crawl under the flowered down comforter as soon as I return to the room.

A Summer Thursday

When I arrive at the beach house, Jaytee greets me with unbounded enthusiasm. "Judy, you are here!" He runs to me and wants to have a conversation, but doesn't know what else to say, so I talk to him for a while, and ask him if he knows any finger songs. I sing the "Itsy Bitsy Spider" and his eyes light up.

"Sing it again!" he says. He knows the song. His hands, however, remain at his sides. "Again!"

David is also happy to see me. He tells me he'd like to get a limousine with a driver, and then he and I could go someplace together.

"Oh, gosh, no limousines at the beach!" I respond lightly, but touched by his idea.

Janie and Maureen are geared up, with Alily's help, for another day at the beach with the children, as well as a trip to a nearby souvenir shop. I'm beginning to understand the tradeoff here. Beth pays for the beach house. Maureen and Janie get a week at the beach in exchange for grocery shopping and helping with child care, which provides Beth with a little bit of a break.

Late morning Beth and I leave for a town nearby to do some shopping for Shontel's seventh birthday. As we stroll through the toy department of a large store, she sees many things she wants to buy for Shontel, plus she sees toys she'd like to buy for Jaytee and Jeffrey. It's not the birthday week for those boys, though, and finally settles on several gifts for Shontel: a four-foot long foam glider that will be perfect for the beach, a SpongeBob SquarePants card game, and a sleeping bag with a blue frog design that comes in a backpack with a flashlight and water bottle – perfect for sleepovers. In the bakery department, she has a cake decorated with Shontel's name.

Birthday business taken care of, we move on to a souvenir store where Beth knows there are a lot of giraffe items. I learn that Trina has a twenty-one-year-old sister, who supervises visits between Trina and her mother. Later this year, when the sister has moved into a bigger apartment, she will become Trina's guardian. The sister loves giraffes, and Beth wants her to have a souvenir from the beach. *As if Beth's plate isn't full enough*, I think.

Next we find a seafood restaurant for a last lunch. I'll be driving home the next day. Although it's busy and we have to wait to be seated, we don't mind: it's more time to talk. Eventually we get a table looking right out onto the bay. While we wait for our food, Beth asks me about my days since I retired from teaching.

"I'm so used to being busy; I have trouble imagining retirement." she says.

We talk about the town where we grew up, and I learn something new about how she paid for college. Besides two scholarships, one from the nursing school and one from the county medical association, an old bachelor rancher who ate his dinners nightly in the cafe gave her mom money for her tuition. She barely knew the man, but her mother had talked about her daughter over the years while serving his supper.

"It wasn't that much." she says. "Nursing school was inexpensive then. We had free housing and food in exchange for working in the hospital as aides a certain number of hours per week, and we could work extra hours for pay. Still, I couldn't have done it without his help."

"What about the fall?" I ask.

In late September, she's joining other longtime friends who are or have been foster moms for an annual weekend away at a bed and breakfast, so arranging care for everyone will be a priority when she gets back to Sylvia Street.

"We've also got some some "shopping" appointments, where I can take the kids to the nonprofit agency that has donations of new clothes, shoes, coats, and backpacks for foster kids. Trina will be starting high school, and she's registered at a public alternative school." She takes a drink of Diet Pepsi and continues. "Markie will be back in life and work skills classes. Mercedes will continue in therapy and have a tutor provided by the school district, maybe someone more dependable this year." She rolls her eyes. "Hopefully, her platelet issues will resolve with changes to her medication. Jaytee will return to Head Start, and Shontel will enter second grade. They are doing a home study on that 'mom'that proved disastrous in May, and the children could possibly go back to the Midwest again." I can tell on Beth's face that she doesn't want to dwell on that possibility.

I'm feeling overwhelmed by the decisions ahead, but she continues, "Maybe there will movement in Jeffrey's situation. In the meantime his supervised visits and speech therapy sessions will continue. When Trina's sister has demonstrated to the state that she is capable, by keeping her new job, she will become the girl's guardian".

Despite feeling full of both seafood and information, I want to hear more, but after several hours we decide we need to leave. We make sure to leave a generous tip for the waitress who has probably stayed past her lunch shift.

When we arrive at the house, Maureen and Janie have just returned from the souvenir store, and Janie has a gift for me. Remembering our conversation about the expensive bracelet with the book quote, she hands me a refrigerator magnet that says "Yay! Books!" It's just a magnet, but I am again moved by the spirit of generosity I see in this whole group.

Coleen missed the trip to the souvenir store because she was napping, and now she's upset. I suspect she did not hear the earlier conversation, and didn't know the trip was planned. I feel badly that she missed this opportunity because of her hearing issues, so I offer to run her to the store. Beth gives her money from the girl's account and we're off.

She browses for a long time, looking at most everything in the store and I make a point of going my own way, doing my own browsing. When she comes to the counter, I move close just in case she needs my help.

The cashier says "How you doin'?" But Coleen doesn't answer because she isn't looking at him and doesn't hear him. He gives her an unkind glare.

"She probably didn't hear you," I say. "She's mostly deaf."

"Oh," he says, relieved. His face softens. After he rings up her purchases, a necklace, a shirt, a bracelet, a craft book, and a hat, he turns the calculator so she can see the total. It's over fifty dollars and she only has forty dollars, money Beth had given her from the girl's account. She doesn't know what to do. I suddenly realize that her practical number sense is very weak. For a moment, I consider covering the difference, but decide not to. We check the individual price tags, and the cashier and I group the items in various ways. She decides on a combination that turns out to be just over forty dollars.

"Don't bother about the eleven cents", the man says to me. I think Coleen wonders why she didn't get some change. He bags the shirt and craft book, and we drive back to the house. When I park the car, I turn and compliment her on her decision to buy the book. It has clear pages with intricate stained glass-like designs and a package of colored markers.

When we return to the house Beth is kneading dough. There's a certain buzz in the air. The family likes her homemade pizza.

Meanwhile, Coleen starts filling in a page in her new book, Jaytee plays engineer, and Shontel sits on top of a pile of sofa pillows pretending to be on a throne with her new stuffed raccoon. Jeffrey vocalizes at a high pitch and tries to get into the kitchen cupboards. Beth yells for Alily to do something with him. Meanwhile, across the room, David is loudly singing to no one in particular, "Judy is so gorgeous. I like Judy." Markie asks questions about pizza toppings. Mercedes sits in the middle of it all, reading.

Beth then makes a cooking mistake; thinking of parchment baking paper, she inadvertently lines the pizza pans with waxed paper. The first two pizzas have paper baked into the crust and diners have to peel it off in small pieces as they eat. Removing the rolled-out dough and toppings from the paper on the unbaked pans creates a mess because the dough clings to the waxed paper. Beth is frustrated beyond belief. She doesn't verbalize her frustration, but it is on her face, and for a few minutes she doesn't talk or respond to any child's request. Because she's so capable and calm in a household that is often kind of crazy, this is a side of her I haven't seen before. I'm almost relieved to see her so discombobulated!

The calamity is short lived, though, and everybody gets his or her fill of either white-sauce vegetarian pizza with vegetables, or traditional pepperoni pizza with red sauce. Soon, however, another small crisis erupts. It's Markie's turn to do dishes, and she doesn't know how to work this particular dishwasher, so she gets angry and storms out of the kitchen. I know better than to do her work: it needs to be waiting for her when she cools down, which she eventually does. Beth has told me her temper used to be worse. In middle school, she had issues with getting angry and scratching or kicking her teachers and aides. Right before I leave for the inn, she has returned to the kitchen.

Back in my room, I fold up a piece of watercolor paper and paint a cake and seven candles on it for Shontel. I'll give it to her, along with the frog bookmark I bought for her earlier today, when I stop by to say goodbye to everyone in the morning.

A Summer Friday

AFTER ANOTHER BREAKFAST of toaster biscuits, fresh raspberries, and elk viewing, I check out of the inn and head back to the beach house. Shontel has been permitted to open one of her birthday presents, the glider that is almost as long as she is tall. Janie and Aurora help her assemble it so that they can fly it off the deck. The sun is starting to burn off the fog, and there is just a tiny breeze. It should be a good day for a glider. Jaytee and Jeffrey are playing quietly while Beth is enjoying a morning Diet Pepsi. The older girls and boys are still asleep. I give Shontel her card and bookmark, and she says a quick thanks. The glider has captured most of her attention, though, and she returns to its construction after a polite minute with me. I say my goodbyes to those in the room.

The trip back to my own house will take several hours, but I don't need the radio today; recalling the events of the week, the conversations, the frustrations and struggles, the laughter, the good food, and the magnificence of the surf will keep me company all the way home.

FALL

OVER THE RIVER AND
THROUGH THE WOODS

EARLY THANKSGIVING MORNING the freeway is not crowded, and I'm excited to be on my way to Sylvia Street. I haven't seen the family since I left the beach in August, and although email correspondence with Beth has kept me someone abreast of what's been happening, I'm looking forward to seeing everyone.

I've been preparing for this trip for several days. I have purchased and wrapped Christmas presents for each of them. For the older girls, who all like crafts, I found little unfinished wooden boxes with hinged lids, a bottle of Mod-Podge (glue and matte finish), and several foam brushes. With magazine photos, tissue paper, or copies of photos, they can decorate their boxes collage style. I also got each of them a little case for their ear buds. For David, I found a seven-inch battery-operated vacuum cleaner designed for keyboards and other electronics. For Shontel, I found a colorful nonfiction book about sea life filled with photos and narrated by SpongeBob SquarePants. For the little ones I got a toy broom, toy mop, whisk broom and dustpan. The gifts are all in a big bag Beth can store in her closet or under her bed for a month. I baked a batch of peanut butter cookies and a loaf of cranberry bread and bought cheese, salami, and baked pita chips. I packed a large bag of satsumas and a package of sugar snap peas and baby carrots. Assembling all of this reminded me of Beth's explanation of vacations: part of the joy of a vacation is the planning and anticipation.

As I drive, I think about the updates Beth shared with me this fall about the family. Jeffrey is still living with her. His birth mom dropped his little sister, and for a short while, she joined the household on Sylvia Street. Mom blamed the incident on a bad reaction to methadone and cough medicine. Now the grandmother, who lives with the mom, is responsible. Because the girl is basically healthy, and doesn't need a complicated nutritional regimen and regular speech therapy like her brother, the birth household can manage. Jeffrey's needs are another issue, and his mother is still regularly missing her visitation appointments.

Jaytee's challenges at Head Start have been increasing, and Beth thinks he might need to be medicated in order to socialize and learn. She commented that she doesn't like to have kids on behavioral prescriptions before they are school age, but his daily struggles might make this necessary. His sister Shontel has also had a hard time of it. Her behavior since returning from the adoptive family in the Midwest has continued to be an issue. Beth held discussions with her teacher; the girl was continually missing recess for not completing her work. Because Shontel has an identified attention deficit disorder, partly but not completely managed medication, insisting she miss recess to do her work is not permitted by disability law.

Trina started high school at an alternative school in September. But this week, two days before her birthday and four days before Thanksgiving, Beth was notified that Trina would be moving in with her sister and changing schools. With only one day's notice before the change was to take effect, Beth dropped her plans for the day to bake a birthday cake, wrap birthday presents and a sock monkey, and fix a birthday dinner. For Beth, these sudden changes in circumstances are nothing new, but I am disappointed that I won't see Trina this trip.

Mercedes is enrolled in school for two classes before going to dialysis midday, and therefore is up and on the school bus each morning. As I drive I wonder as I drive if she's been in contact with her dad or his ex-girlfriend. I wonder if she's still having seizures. Beth says they have decreased in frequency. She also tells me Mercedes is developing a warmer relationship with the little ones. I want to see that. There's no news about Markie, Coleen, or David.

In late September, Beth had a getaway weekend with long-time friends who are, or were until retirement, nurses and foster moms for medically fragile kids. The group stayed at a bed and breakfast out on the coast, as they have done for years. Nadine's mom, who for several years worked for Beth as a regular helper before she moved to a different city, came to stay with the kids. Since August, Beth has read several books and found a new line dancing class with a really good teacher who teaches a wealth of dances.

∾

As I DRIVE to Beth's house, I notice the snowy mountains are "out", as we say in the Northwest, or, in other words, are not hidden in an overcast sky. Golden leaves of trees grace the riverbank below a rare blue sky, and just a hint of low lying fog hangs a few feet above the river. Trite as is sounds, I can't help but sing to myself, "Over the river and through the woods..."

Midway, I stop at a friend's house for a few minutes. She takes a break from chopping vegetables for her Thanksgiving feast, and we share a cup of coffee at her kitchen table. When I tell her about the gifts I'm taking, she suggests that I give them to the kids to open while I'm there, so they'll know who they're from. "They might not remember you in December," she says.

"Oh, they'll remember me!" I respond, but when I'm on the road again, I start to doubt myself. What if they don't?

A November Thursday

Sure enough, when I pull up to the house a turkey flag is hanging over the front porch. A young teen I have never seen before is sailing through the air on a rope swing attached to a tree in the front yard. "Hi, I'm Judy, Beth's friend. Are you connected to the people in this house?"

"I'm with Maureen," she says. Before I even enter the house and get the details, I see that yet again, the household has embraced another person.

Jeffrey gives me what might be the world's largest grin, and Jaytee exclaims, "Judy, Judy, Judy!"

David immediately asks me four questions: "Are you staying with us? How long are you staying? How is your car doing? How often do you vacuum your car?" I think to myself that I should have vacuumed it before the trip. He'll be disappointed if he sees the leaf litter on my floor mats.

Markie comes out of the kitchen and greets me warmly. I put the bag of pita chips on the counter with the cheese and crackers already sitting out. No one has had pita chips before. David especially wonders how they taste. He has no concerns about the peanut butter cookies. He *knows* he loves them. He and Jaytee and Markie take care of all the foods I bought. Maureen waves a hello from across the room, where she's wiping off the dining table, and her boys each give me a tiny nod of the head that I take as enough for a greeting, given their ages. I offer Maureen the jar of strawberry jam I made in the summer as a gift for her gracious-ness in August. She introduces me to Jean, the girl on the rope swing. Her long bangs hide much of her face when her head is tipped down, and we can't really make eye contact, but she says hello. I want to ask how she fits into this group, but decide to wait, assuming I will hear the explanation later. Beth has been play-ing with Jeffrey on the couch. She mentions that they've just had snacks to hold them until a midafternoon Thanksgiving meal, and to help myself.

Beth suggests that the little ones need some fresh air. Maureen agrees, and takes the baby, Jaytee, Shontel, her two boys, and Jean to a park within walking distance. The Thanksgiving meal is underway and under control so Beth and I have a few minutes to talk. She explains that Jean's mother, a single Mom and friend of Maureen, suffers from mental illness, and the girl spends part of every week with Maureen. She's not a legal guardian; it's an informal arrangement that has developed out of the friendship between the two moms. Shortly after she finishes telling me Jean's story, the group returns with rosy cheeks and bright eyes.

Alily arrives and the household is excited to see her. "We're just going to play cards," Maureen says. "Come join us." Alily pulls a chair up to the table. Beth retrieves a shoebox from a high cup-board that has several Uno decks and several sets of playing cards.

Before she sits down to play, she holds up a plastic sandwich bag of playing cards labeled "Almost a full deck" and says to me, "Yup, describes us pretty well!"

The group plays Uno for several rounds. Markie calls "Uno" one play too late, and when people complain about it, she responds, "But I didn't notice until now!" After a few more rounds, they move on to a game of spoons, and Markie seems to have improved her skills with this game.

I'm just an observer, sitting at the other end of the oblong table, until Shontel asks me to play Go Fish with her using extra Uno cards. It's not clear to me how the game will come to an end, or how a winner will be declared, but we play anyway. When she doesn't have a yellow six, she puts down a four and a two together, and I think, *You go, girl!*

Mercedes comes up from downstairs and seems both surprised and pleased to see me. "Hi, Judy," she says, putting a hand of my shoulder. She sits down at the table and I excuse myself from the card game with Shontel to give her my full attention.

"You look good, Mercedes. How have you been doing?" I ask.

She shrugs and smiles seemingly pleased that I notice. "Pretty good. I was in the hospital for a week. I needed a new port for my dialysis."

"Did you talk with the dialysis center about getting heated beds like they had at Astoria that you so enjoyed?"

"Yea," Mercedes says with a frown, "but they said it's too expensive."

"Oh, that's too bad. It seems like it would make so much better. I hear you're in school."

"I'm in English and Algebra every morning. They want to add history, but I don't want to take history. Let's play Go Fish". She deals regular, not Uno cards, and we play several rounds. This is more interaction of any kind than I had with her in March, May, and August put together. She's healthier, I think, and more confident. Maybe maturity is part of it.

Throughout this whole time, Jeffrey, happy as can be, has been playing on the floor with a bike helmet, a doll carrier, and a skate-board. He puts the bike helmet in the carrier and lifts the carrier onto the skate-board. He rolls his collection a foot or two, and then he disassembles the whole thing and starts again. Jaytee has been sitting calmly and quietly under the dining table throwing cards over his head.

Beth extracts herself from the card games to finish dinner preparations. She calmly mashes the potatoes, makes gravy, and puts homemade yeast rolls she baked yesterday in the oven to warm. When she opens the overflowing refrigerator, a very-full pitcher falls of strawberry lemonade spills across the kitchen floor. Beth mutters and mops up the sticky mess. Like the waxed paper and pizza incident at the beach, it's a wonderfully human moment in a kitchen that sometimes seems too well organized to be real.

Coleen sets up the card table, and extra chairs are brought from bedrooms. This movement of furniture momentarily disorients both David and Jaytee, but they recover quickly. Mercedes and Maureen set the table, complete with a white lace table cloth for the big table and placements for the card table. There are stemmed goblets for sparkling cranberry juice and sparkling cider for everyone except Jeffrey.

Around two-thirty, we gather for dinner. Beth leads everyone in signing and saying grace. Jeffrey signs the amen. As Mercedes passes me a large bowl after serving herself, she explains to me that she can eat these mashed potatoes because they soaked overnight before being cooked. When Beth asks each person what they're grateful for, several people respond with the word family. Beth is grateful that she'll never run out of books. Shontel's response is my favorite: "I'm grateful that I haven't gotten in trouble all day today."

David calls the sparkling juice wine, and he wonders if it's the same wine his pastor uses for communion. That reminds him of his long-held wish, and he whispers to me "I want the pastor and mom to get married." I think he knows that this comment, often repeated, makes Beth roll her eyes.

At the card table, Maureen's son is having a much simpler dinner than the rest of us. He has four dinner rolls, a jar of peanut butter, a jar of jam, and a knife. For the rest of us, in addition to turkey, potatoes and gravy, there is moist stuffing from the turkey, and pan-baked bread dressing. There are two kinds of pickles and two kinds of olives. Puzzling to several of the children, there are brined cherries that taste like olives. Several cooked vegetables and real butter for the rolls complete the meal. Only one goblet of cider spills during dinner, and it's barely noticed. David suddenly realizes that it's three o'clock. He swivels in his chair to the nearby computer and turns it on so he can watch a PBS Kids show. Beth reminds him that we're in the middle of a holiday meal and asks him to turn it off.

When the meal ends, Mercedes and Maureen clear the dishes while Beth whips the cream for pie. Jeffrey gets mostly whipped cream with a little bit of pumpkin pie. He eats it with both a spoon and with his hands. Getting adequate nutrition remains a challenge for him. He is still on a high-calorie formula that must be prepared with a high degree of precision. Once mixed, it is only good for a short while. Beth tells me that earlier in the month they tried to switch him to another formula that was simpler to mix, and could be stored longer in the refrigerator, a necessity if Jeffrey is ever to successfully live with his father and thrive. Unfortunately, his body could not tolerate the new formula, and it made him very sick. Today, though, he is not sick, and is really enjoying his bowl of whipped cream.

Markie is surprisingly upbeat about dish duty today. It will be more than one load, so she gets started right away. When the first load is done, I help empty the dishwasher, and we chat. She explains the features of the new refrigerator, and shows me how the water dispenser on the front can be locked, an important feature with Jaytee in the house. She also explains that her mom doesn't like the replacement refrigerator because it doesn't have enough space for all the food they need. The configuration of space is narrow and deep so food must be stored behind other food. When I ask Beth about it later, she explains that her old refrigerator broke under warranty, but the only replacement with a water dispenser on the front that would fit in her space was this particular model, which, because of its narrow shelves, does not work for a busy household with lots of teen and young adult use; it's hard to find and remove foods tucked at the back.

Jaytee is actually looking at the "search and find" book I brought as a gift. Like an *I Spy* book, the detailed photographs and lists of items to find offer many reasons to pour over the pages. Without realizing it, I picked the right book, because it's full of toy trains, which both little boys love. Jaytee wants to talk to me about the trains while Jeffrey builds a train with DuPlo bricks (a toddler's version of Legos) under the table. David asks Coleen to find him a Christmas movie on TV. Eventually, Jaytee wonders away, and Maureen and Beth and I sit at the table and talk. Maureen tells us about the fundraising event she headed up last month. The spaghetti feed and silent auction helped her raise thousands of dollars for a friend fighting brain cancer.

While we chat, Coleen checks her phone and with a stomp of her foot, voices a frustration. With a combination of signs and words, she tells Beth that her birth mother hasn't texted a response to the happy Thanksgiving message she sent hours earlier.

Her birth mother? I think. I had no idea that Coleen was in touch with her.

When Coleen returns to the living room to watch TV with David, I ask Beth, and she tells more of Coleen's story. Her parents already had a rocky marriage before Coleen and her sister were born. They were poor, and the husband was difficult and perhaps abusive. They were overwhelmed dealing with a one-year-old baby boy and Coleen's premature sister, so they rarely visited the hospital to see Coleen and essentially failed to bond with her. She remained in the hospital a full three months and then, still fragile, deaf, and needing more careful tending than a healthy full-term baby, was sent home. Beth points out that the young family was not provided with any sort of assistance. Not surprisingly, twenty-four hours later the parents returned her to the hospital and said they couldn't handle her. They released her to foster care, and she went home to Beth. Sporadic visits over the next two years didn't improve the bond between parents and child.

"I think the father resented having case workers in his life. You know, felt they were poking around too much. Probably at his insistence, when Coleen was two, they gave her up for adoption."

Five or six years later, and now divorced, the mom, working as a taxi driver, was assigned a daily pick up of a foster child living on Sylvia Street for delivery to a special school across town. Recognizing the address, she reconnected with Beth and Coleen. Throughout the years, contact has been spotty: new marriages, moves, and changes in phone numbers have all made the relationship difficult. Nevertheless, Coleen knows her mom, her brother, and her twin sister, who now has a baby and a boyfriend. Messy and imperfect as it is, I'm thrilled to learn that she knows her biological family. It's a good Thanksgiving story for me today.

Beth seems relaxed and talkative. She reminisces about an eight-year-old girl late one night years ago.

"I'm thinking tonight for some reason about Desiree. It was wintertime and cold, but she was wearing flip flops on her very dirty feet and an adult woman's cotton sleeveless dress that had been cut off at the bottom and a filthy sweatshirt. Her father had locked her out that night, and someone in the trailer park had called the authorities. They brought her to my house at around midnight."

Beth bathed her, washed and unsnarled her tangled hair, and found pajamas and school clothes for the next day in her big closet.

"When I took the girl to her school the next morning, I accompanied her to the classroom to meet the teacher. For a few minutes, the teacher didn't recognize Desiree; he was just visibly overcome by the beautiful little girl standing in front of him." Desiree was not medically fragile, just fragile, and she didn't stay on Sylvia for long. She didn't need nursing, just nurturing.

SHONTEL TELLS BETH that she'd like to play her violin. Beth gets it from her own bedroom, where it is safely stored out of Jaytee's reach. "I need help with the song, Mom." the girl explains.

"You mean you want me to sing with you? What song?"

"Jingle Bells." she responds, placing her tiny violin under her chin and arranging her fingers. Together they start the song. Shontel plays a single clear note through the whole sing, with bow strokes in perfect time to "Jingles Bells." Everyone claps. I compliment her on the clear tone. She's working hard to keep her face as neutral as possible but she can't veil the pride showing in her eyes. Maybe she's slightly embarrassed by the attention. The concert over, she carefully places the school-issued violin back in its case while Beth explains that a grant has allowed all of the early primary students at the neighborhood school to have violin class twice a week.

Next Shontel and the other kids drag a tub of Bristle Blocks and Duplo bricks to the center of the room and spread out on the carpet to build things. Beth calls my attention to Jeffrey who, while making machine sounds, "vacuums" the end table with a Duplo vacuum cleaner he has built. He may be in the fifth percentile for size, and his vocabulary may include only one word, but he can build a cleaning machine! Jaytee seems unable to construct anything, but asks me to build him an airplane which he then flies around the room for twenty minutes. Shontel wants my help building a castle. We have only enough pieces for a small three-walled castle with no roof, but she's content and talks to herself as we build.

After a snack of cheese, pita chips, (which are a hit with Jaytee but no one else) and a little pie, it's bedtime for the little ones. Jaytee is proud of his new toothbrush and shows it to everyone. It doesn't taste good to him, though, because he has put soap on it, so Beth helps him rinse it off and use toothpaste instead.

David talks about what a busy day he will have tomorrow. There is both recycling to put out and his outdoor Christmas decorations to put up. Alily is spending the night. Maureen and her boys leave for their motel. I decide to do the same, and when I say goodnight, David asks me if I'm coming back tomorrow. When I say yes, he explains that I'll see his Christmas decorations.

A November Friday

Midmorning I arrive at the house to see Jaytee in Mercedes's lap while the two share a picture book. I think about how she so pointedly ignored the young ones last spring. Now Jaytee is quietly snuggled against her, and she has an arm wrapped around him. To my amazement, they laugh and talk quietly together about the picture on the page.

Shontel has a bump on her forehead; she explains that she and Jaytee have had a tough morning in part because he hurled a toy train engine at her from across the room. Jaytee shows an interest in this conversation and jumps down from Mercedes's lap. I ask Jaytee if I should throw a toy at Beth. He says no; he's shocked by the idea, but I don't think he really understands why I asked the question. He says matter-of-factly and without remorse, "I throw the train." Jaytee never uses past tense or future tense. Everything he says is in present tense, like, "I go to dentist" or "We go to the beach and ride the train." Beth generally repeats what he has said in the proper tense before responding. Shontel knows better than to expect an apology even from a calm Jaytee, and goes off to play.

I realize that I haven't looked at the Christmas decorations in the yard and that David will be disappointed if I don't comment, so I go back outside to look. There is a Santa flag hanging above the porch, and next to the steps, an electric snowflake the size of a large dinner plate is staked to the ground. Next to it stands a reindeer the size of a Chihuahua with a red bulb nose and lights on its harness. David has a remote switch, so that he can turn the snow-flake and the reindeer on and off from inside the house. I don't know what I was expecting, but the snowflake and Chihuahua Rudolph that stand shin high were not it! I have to think of what I will say if he asks me about them.

Alily fixes lunch for the little ones. Beth has been working on her Christmas cards but now she reminds Mercedes that it's about time to leave for dialysis. She gets her book, iPod, and blanket, and they leave.

David has finished a late breakfast and comes over to the couch. "Oh what am I going to do with you Judy? You need to move here. I really like you Judy. Judy, you should live here, or in Jamaica, or in Japan! Is there carpet on your stairs?"

How to respond? "No carpet on my stairs. They're wooden slabs."

"Oh, that's too bad." I think he would like to come and vacuum them.

Maureen, Jean, and the boys arrive after a morning of swimming at their hotel. They're hungry, and choose their grandma's rolls with peanut butter and jelly. Maureen puts a bag of T-shirts from her fundraiser on the table. Soon her friend Janie arrives, and the three of us sort through the shirts. Janie buys several. I buy one that shows a woman delivering a martial arts kick to the word cancer.

When Beth returns, Maureen brings in several large bags of Christmas presents for the household. She and Beth whisk them into the bedroom without drawing the little ones' attention. Come Christmas, Maureen will be east of the mountains with her children's other grandparents. When they come out of the bedroom, Maureen, walking behind her mother, is laughing. "I can't believe my mother is wearing jeans with sequin bling on the butt!"

"They're the only kind I could find," Beth mutters.

Jeffrey is taking a nap, but Jaytee has decided to take a whistle and blow it loudly in front of Jeffrey's door, a no-no for sure. Beth quickly leads him to the other side of room and confiscates the whistle. "I'm mad," she says to him, "because that that was the wrong thing to do."

He tries to get close to her. When he's remorseful, she doesn't immediately give him comfort. She very purposely turns her attention to other things. It isn't that he needed to blow the whistle to get her attention. Moments before, he was sitting on her lap while she explained the engine, the coal car, the crane car, freight car, log car, and caboose in a train book.

After five minutes have passed, she tells him he can't blow the whistle by Jeffrey's door when he's napping. "Do you know why?" she asks.

"It wake up Jeffrey."

"Right," she says. "That was an impulse. When you have an impulse, you need to stop, and think, 'should I do this?' " Her lowered eyebrows stress the importance of saying this and, at the same time, the kindness showing in her eyes themselves reveal the hopelessness of saying it. I think of what Susan said last summer over coffee at Starbucks: that kids like her foster grandson and Jaytee need an angel on their shoulder. Beth gives him a Jaytee a hug, and he gets down to play with a train on the floor. It is just not his day.

Just then Shontel yells from her room, "I don't want to make my bed!"

"That's your job," Beth responds.

"But not four times!" comes the retort. Jaytee has rumpled her bed into a nest several times throughout the morning. He likes to make a nest of blankets and sit in it with stuffed animals.

"I'll come help you make it again, okay?" Beth says quietly and gets up.

"While I ponder Beth's seemingly endless reserves of patience with these two, Markie comes over to the table with a notebook and pencil. "Remember last summer when you were telling Mama about the new things you try to do each year that add up to your age?" I'm stunned not only that she remembers the conversation but that she can restate the concept. "My birthday is coming soon, and I'll be twenty-one." She continues. "I want to do twenty-one new things this year, but I don't remember what categories to use. Can you write them down for me?"

We discuss categories and I share that I have new books I've read on my list. She says, "I listen to books on CD from the library. Let's put 'books listened to.'" When I tell her I put new foods tried on my list, she says, "Oh, that's a good one for me! I'm not very brave about new foods." I also tell her I include new places I have visited on my list. She thinks for a minute, and then explains that she can't find new places on the public bus by herself, but if she takes the route with a teacher a few times, she's fine. "How about if we put 'new bus routes?'" After we discuss it, she also adds new words and new friends to the list. "I like both of those!" she grins.

During this year, Markie's goal is to listen to three or four books on tape, try four or five new foods, take maybe four or five new bus routes, learn four new words, and make four new friends. She'll keep track of them in the notebook, and add them up to total twenty-one. This will be big math for her. I try to lay out the page to make it as clear as possible.

I ask Markie what kind of work placement her school is giving her this year, and she explains that two days a week she takes a bus to a greenhouse where she has learned to transplant seedling. "Do you like it?" I ask.

"Yeah, it's okay, but it's not what I want to do. You know, I really want to work with animals." She says nodding her head vigorously.

While I chat with Markie, I see David is in the entryway doing his daily exercises. It must be one o'clock! He's making large sideways scissor steps back and forth while bracing himself against the wall. The stretching helps him maintain some flexibility and strength and keeps his leg muscles from stiffening and contracting. Most of the time he straps braces on his lower legs for added support.

Later that afternoon, Trina arrives for a visit. She's been shopping with her sister and mom in the early morning to catch black friday sales, and she's wearing a new winter coat and new pants. Trina seems truly happy to see people, and they to see her. Maureen's son Travis comes and sits next to her. He idolizes Trina and hangs on her every word.

Maureen asks about her living situation. "Your guardian is a twenty-something? Is that sweet or what?"

Beth tells Trina, "Go wake up Alily. She is still asleep."

"She's here, too?" Trina asks with delight, and heads downstairs. Alily, Mercedes, Coleen and Trina visit and snack together for about an hour.

Later, when she's ready to leave, Trina asks Beth for bus money "What about your bus pass?"

"I can't find it," she answers. This might be a scan to get a little extra cash, but it might be the truth. Trina is notoriously messy and has trouble keeping track of her stuff. Beth sighs and goes to get her purse.

I leave mid-afternoon to meet an old friend for dinner. Turning my attention to my former college roommate will not be easy. My mind is full, thinking about how Maureen is so much like her mother, and marveling at my conversations with both Mercedes and Markie.

A November Saturday

I ARRIVE SATURDAY morning just as Markie announces that her sheets are out of the washer, and it's David's turn. Here's another part of the household structure: the older ones all wash their own sheets on Saturday. I suspect Markie and David always have their bedding done before Mercedes and Coleen are even out of bed.

Comfortably resting in the recliner, Beth is addressing more of her Christmas cards. After David starts the washer, he comes back to talk with her about his upcoming birthday. He'd like a big party. She explains to me that they sometimes have a Christmas open house the Sunday before Christmas, and this year David's birthday falls on that Sunday.

Turning to David, she says, "Perhaps your birthday party can be part of the open house like it was a few years ago."

Nodding, he states firmly, "and I want a chocolate cake." With an abrupt change of subject, he asks, "Markie when will you be moving out to your own apartment?

She says with exasperation, "I keep telling you. Mama and I have to talk about that!" That seems to end the conversation, and both young adults leave the room.

Working on her cards and visiting at the same time is no problem for Beth, so I mention that Mercedes seems healthier. She tells me about the infection in her catheter port that hospitalized her earlier in the fall. The infection had spread throughout her body, and in addition to clearing up the infection with IV antibiotics, installing a new catheter on the other side of her chest was necessary.

"Being in the hospital too long isn't good for Mercedes." Beth says. "The nurses ask her how she feels and she says she feels crummy. Of course she does. They wait on her. She doesn't have to do school work. Once her infection cleared up, staying in the hospital wasn't helping her." She adds that it's important for Mercedes to learn to cope with the fact that she feels pretty rotten most of the time. While someone else might have appreciated a week's relief from caring for Mercedes, Beth was worried about the girl letting her medical issues define her.

Mercedes is generally healthier than she was in the summer, but maintaining her well-being is an incredible balancing act for her medical team. The doctors have taken her off some of the prescriptions she was on, including prophylactic antivirals and antibiotics, because the side effects were creating their own problems. I wonder if this contributed to her runaway infection in the fall.

Throughout our conversation, Jeffrey has been playing happily with a shoelace and a comb. When he's hungry, he tugs on Beth to get her attention, moves his high chair, and signs "more".

She says, "Okay you're hungry." She signs "hungry" and puts him in the high chair. "More what?" she asks and signs, "Cheese? crackers? noodles? yogurt? Tell me."

His response is "uh, uh, uh." She sighs and fixes his lunch. It's a bowl of mashed potatoes with a little gravy, and maybe a little pumpkin pie filling, which he eats with a spoon and with his fingers.

Because Alily is there and willing to babysit, Beth and I leave to join a friend we know from childhood for lunch at a nearby restaurant. We laugh and talk about books, politics, religion, and childhood memories, and suddenly two hours have passed. It feels like twenty minutes.

Not only that, my short visit has gone by too quickly. I'm developing an incredible fondness for the kids on Sylvia Street. When we return to the house, Coleen is out in front yard.

"Where are you going?" she asks, as I unlock and open my car door.

"Home. I'm driving home today."

"Don't go!" she says. "We like you here. Mama likes you here."

I am moved not only by what she says, but also by the fact that she initiated and held a conversation with me! Once again, my drive home has my mind in a whirl about what I've experienced these last few days. Who needs music on the radio? I replay in my head listening to the violin solo, buying the kick cancer t-shirt, watching the Duplo vacuum cleaner in action, receiving the suggestion I move to Jamaica or Japan, helping build the list of twenty-one new things, laughing at the soapy toothbrush, and treasuring the lovely Thanksgiving moment of gratitude: "I'm thankful I haven't gotten in trouble all day." It's been a wonderful Thanksgiving.

WINTER

The Basketball Gym

I HAVE A *chance to see Eli, a young friend of mine who plays collegiate basketball, when his team has a game on this side of the mountains. Before the game, his parents treat me and several family friends to dinner at a pan-Asian restaurant. We gather around a large table and order family style. As the lazy Susan in the middle of the table rotates so that we can serve ourselves to the delicious curries and stir-fry dishes, the thought crosses my mind that Beth needs one of these on her dining table. On second thought, though, I realize that Jaytee and Jeffrey would probably love the opportunity to learn about centrifugal force by experimenting with it. I envision food splattered on the wall and toys flying through the air. Maybe a lazy Susan is not such a good idea.*

I get to the gym before the other. While I watch the players warm up, I think about my visit tomorrow to Beth's house. A few weeks ago I emailed her to tell her to arrange for a visit.

"I need to see what flag hangs from your porch in January," I tell her. This time she offers to let me stay at the house. "Where?" I ask. "Your bedrooms are full."

"I'll rent Shontel's room from her." It seems that they're negotiating the price; Shontel has said that she wants either a quarter or a dollar a night.

The old cliché crosses my mind: A bargain at any price.

Soon my dinner companions arrive at the arena, and the evening's event begins. When the players are introduced, Eli is the only one who shakes hands with the referees and the other coaches. My heart is proud and melts just a little. It's not an ingratiating move. He's six feet seven inches of earnestness and heart.

Eli doesn't have a perfect game, but makes some crucial defensive plays. Although he misses a free throw, he arches a lovely three pointer near the end of the very close game. Eli, as well as the rest of the players are graceful, alert, and focused.

With the Sylvia Street children on my mind, I think about the gifts these boys have received: good health, strong coordinated bodies, and intelligent minds that can handle both the academic rigor of college and the regimen of basketball.

After the game, I notice a young adult man walking awkwardly alone in large circles around the court. He holds up a small yellow toy truck and talks to it. His gait, facial features, and complete disregard for, or perhaps lack of awareness of, the other people in the gym make me wonder, Who let him? and then I think about Beth. If she were his foster mom and he loved basketball, she'd get him to that arena and allow him to walk around on the court after the game talking to a toy truck. I'm being changed by my observations on Sylvia Street.

When boys exit the locker room, Eli greets his family and personal fans. There are hugs all around, and lots of cameras snapping. Some of his high school buddies from nearby colleges have come to see him play. They have life-size photos of Eli's head on sticks. I realize that Eli not only has family; he has an incredible support network of people who care about him. I'm wishing that all children had this kind of network. Is it Eli's talent and charisma or is it his circumstances and luck of the draw that give him this opportunity?

A January Sunday

"WHAT DO YOU wear to church?" I had asked before the visit.

The answer was a skirt, so this morning I am wearing a skirt when I arrive at the Sylvia Street house. Even though it's January, a Valentine flag hangs on the porch. David is looking forward to the next holiday, I think.

Beth's biggest decision this Sunday morning is whether to take Jeffrey to church. It's clearly more work for her if he goes. David is planning to go, as are Jaytee and Shontel, while the older girls sleep in. Beth could wake Coleen to watch Jeffrey, but she decides in the end to take him along.

We sit in the front pew. David needs to sit up close so he can see, and on the Sundays when Coleen attends, she needs to be close enough to read the pastor's lips.

Shortly after the service begins, everyone gets up to greet one another. The warmth the congregation feels for David, Shontel and Jaytee is clear as they are greeted and hugged. During "time with the youngest," Jaytee and Shontel join the pastor up front to help him string together toy plastic monkeys out of a barrel. These monkeys will be a metaphor in his sermon a few minutes later, but he doesn't explain to the children why they're stringing monkeys. He just thanks them.

Beth has expressed her frustration that there's no Sunday school or nursery. The congregation is small and primarily elderly, and although she herself is connected to many of the members, no other children or youth attend the church. Beth tells me she knows that they the kids are learning that they have a community who cares about them, but she longs for more. She does appreciate David's firm attachment to the church, not only on Sunday morning, but also on Monday when he cleans and has a snack with his girlfriends, as he calls them.

Throughout the service, David quietly hums. Jeffrey, on the other hand, vocalizes at his normal volume, not only during the hymns, but occasionally during the speaking parts of the service. Jaytee and Shontel are amazingly well behaved, partly because when it's time for the sermon, each child gets a lollipop. Sitting between the two of them, I entertain them by drawing on my bulletin and folding a lollipop wrapper into a tiny paper boat.

After church, we go to McDonalds, Jaytee and Shontel's reward for good behavior during the service. While waiting in the drive-thru lane, Beth comments on the sermon we've just heard. The pastor related the story of a cancer-stricken parishioner who prayed for her pain to stop, and for a few hours, it did. It was an example, in his mind, of a listening God. For Beth though, the very idea of a God who would arbitrarily stop or not stop the pain of a suffering person seems unimaginable.

"Are people in pain bad at prayer? Is God that whimsical?" Her voice gets louder and she gestures with her hands. "What about young children in pain?" The more she talks the angrier she gets. The subject changes only because it is time to order Happy Meals.

"Girl or boy Happy Meals?" the attendant asks.

"What's the toy?" Beth inquires.

"Girl or boy meals?" the attendant repeats. When Beth finally learns what the toys are, she chooses two "boy" Happy Meals for both Jaytee and Shontel. Last year Shontel had thrown a fit with the very religious potential adoptive parents, the ones who wanted to change her name and put her in a long dress, when they insisted she take the girly toy at McDonalds.

Back at the house, we eat our lunch at the table, and then David suggests a game of Uno. We play together while Shontel and Beth play Go Fish. When I forget whose turn it is, David says, "Oh, Judy, Judy, beetle juice!" as if to say, "Judy, what am I going to do with you?"

At the other end of the dining table, Beth spreads newspaper so Shontel and Jaytee can paint the little window sun catchers that they received at church this morning. Accompanied by small pots of paint, they are clear plastic pieces designed to look like stained glass. She gets a smock for Jaytee. Shontel works carefully; Jaytee's activity is more random; he just likes using the brush and dipping it in the water. Painting the water cup, the newspaper, and the plastic sun catcher are all equally appealing to him. Eventually his random brush work moves toward a messy accident waiting to happen, and Beth decides he's done painting. Jaytee throws a short tantrum before redirecting his energy into building a blanket nest with a couple of train cars and a stuffed animal.

Then it's show and tell time. Shontel shows me her tent, just big enough for her small body to sleep in. She brings it out into the living room, and Jaytee immediately wants to rough house with it. Beth distracts him, and he asks her for his red toy guitar, which had been taken from him last night because he was misusing it. Both it and the tent are brand new, purchased yesterday with Christmas gift cards from a relative. *A relative?* Wondering who this could be, I make a mental note to ask about it later. Jaytee had enough credit left on his card to also get a pair of Thomas the Tank socks. The socks had not been confiscated for bad behavior, and he proudly shows me his feet.

Getting in on the action, David shows me the stuffed dog Beth gave him for his birthday. Soft and fluffy, it's as long as David is tall, and when I ask, he says that yes, he sleeps with it. He also shows me two pictures books he got for Christmas: one about a man who marries a vacuum cleaner and the other about a little boy who vacuums up his family.

Show and tell over, Beth asks for my help with a project. She needs to draw a floor plan of the house and label not only room dimensions, but also door and window sizes and how far the window sills are from the floor. All smoke alarms and fire extinguisher need to be noted.

Why all this work? Markie becomes an adult soon, and the decision has been made that she will remain on Sylvia Street as a foster adult for the near future. Remaining on Sylvia Street a while longer gives her time to find a job after her schooling finishes without having to adjust to a new living situation at the same time. This will happen, of course, only if the folder full of paperwork for the new license necessary to care for a foster adult can be completed, and this takes time. Among the other requirements, Beth, whose first language is English, must take an English proficiency test. She must also pass a first aid class, even though she's a registered nurse with up-to-date credentials. David and Coleen, as other adults in the home, need to be fingerprinted, and references for Beth need to be listed.

Markie, who has been listening to this conversation, who's been in the house since infancy, and can see the screwiness in this, volunteers, "This is really crazy!"

David's fancy tape measure and a clip-board in hand, Beth and I set off to gather the necessary numbers. In the laundry room, our first stop, there are pieces of clothing and household linens draped and hanging everywhere. Evidently the dryer stopped working last week, and the repairman is not due for another few days. Beth has been limiting herself to one load of laundry a day, and the five containers for dirty laundry are all full. We maneuver around everything to get the measurements, and move on.

The bedrooms in the basement are the most interesting. Coleen's bedroom is an intentional cave. She has a light-blocking fabric covering the window, and the lighting is intentionally dim. David's bedroom is neat as a pin. The only touch of whimsy is a singing bass plaque above his headboard.

When we get to Mercedes's room, she is sitting on the bed beading. Her room is neater and more organized than it was in the spring. I ask her if she's making a bracelet.

"No," she says. "It's a keychain for you, but I'm not finished yet." I am silently overwhelmed.

Markie's room is dizzyingly full. Scarves and swatches of cloth are tacked to the walls in a random pattern almost reminiscent of a crazy quilt. Magazine pictures are thumb tacked over every inch of the ceiling. Extra lamps, furniture, clothes, stuffed animals and trays of plant seedlings from her greenhouse internship fill the room, leaving very little clear floor space. The room measurements are perhaps less accurate for Markie's room because we can't get to the actual walls.

While Beth fixes dinner, I draw a clean floor plan and transfer all the numbers from our rough copy.

David asks about the containers of peanut butter cookies and brownies on the kitchen counter. I explain that I baked them for the household.

"You're like the grandma we never had!" comments Markie.

Setting the table is Shontel's new responsibility. Because of the laundry situation, there will be no cloth napkins tonight. Shontel rips paper towels off the roll and puts them on the table in a fairly random manner. I fold them into triangles and put them under the forks.

"Why are you doing that?" she asks.

I start to tell her that it makes them fancy, but fancy is not important to Shontel, so I tell her instead, "It makes eating dinner more like a party."

Mercedes comes upstairs for dinner and with a little shyness, gives me my key chain, a metal loop with a blue and white chain of seed beads.

"Thank you so much." I offer, and she watches while I get my keys out and immediately attach this priceless gift.

She then gets the milk and water pitchers and helps deliver serving bowls to the table. Watching her work, I notice that the puffiness in her face and body is gone, thanks to a reduction in the steroid does that used to help control her lupus. I imagine she looks more like the image she's been used to seeing in the mirror her whole life.

She's more talkative, and even says to Jaytee, "Where's my hug?" When he holds up his hands from across the room, she asks, "Over there?" and he comes running to give her a hug.

Markie gets Coleen, and for the first time all day, everyone gathers in one place. We enjoy ham and peas in cream sauce over noodles and an assortment of raw vegetables. Mercedes zeroes in on the sugar snap peas, and Shontel has a lion's share of cucumber slices. Jaytee spills his milk; Jeffrey gags on something and spits up most of what he's eaten. Per usual, Markie reacts in disgust while Beth cleans up the mess; the others ignore it.

After dinner Mercedes clears the table and Markie starts the dishes right away. David finds a *Brady Bunch* episode on his computer, and switches back and forth between that and The Home Shopping Network. There's always a chance they'll be showing a vacuum cleaner or steam cleaner. After a few minutes of screen time, he's up and walking around.

Checking the calendar on the wall, he tells me that my birthday, six months away, will be on a Wednesday this year. He had remembered a November conversation about the date of my birthday. "Judy, tomorrow you and I should take a walk down by the bay." He says, and then after a pause adds in all seriousness, "What's a bay?" I tell him that he has to work tomorrow at the church and that I'm spending the day with Beth. Only later do I realize that I never told him what a bay is.

Shontel, Jaytee, and Jeffrey play for almost an hour without any fighting, tantrums, or accidents. It's calm enough for Beth to watch the last half of a basketball game on television. Bedtime for the little ones in this house is often smoother than I expect it to be, and soon all three of them are asleep: Jeffrey in his crib, Jaytee in his now tentless bed, and Shontel in her birthday sleeping bag inside her brand new tent. Mercedes and David take showers, while Beth, muttering about the long wait for the repairman, rearranges drying clothing and linens.

The house is quiet, and Beth and I each read for a while. I don't stay up too late, though. Beth's day starts early, and if I want to keep up with her, I need my rest in my one-dollar-a-night room!

A JANUARY MONDAY

I HEAR NOISE out in the kitchen at about seven o'clock. Reading the morning paper, Beth sits at the table with toast and a Diet Pepsi. Jaytee plays at her feet. Jeffrey eats breakfast in his high chair while Shontel gets herself a bowl of cereal, Markie fixes herself a frozen waffle, and Mercedes toasts an English muffin.

By seven-thirty, Beth has wrestled Jaytee into clothing, given Mercedes a shot, and helped Shontel with her hair. The child is in a good mood this morning. She keeps repeating, "Rise and shine, everybody. We've got to be happy! Rise and shine!"

Shortly before eight, Markie leaves to catch her bus, and Beth gets Coleen up to watch Jeffrey. It's time to drive Mercedes to the high school for her two morning classes, Jaytee to Head Start, and Shontel to school. Jeffrey is mad because he can't go with the others. He drags his coat over to Beth and tugs on her, signing an adamant "please!"

When we drop Mercedes off, Beth watches her walk up the sidewalk to the front steps of the school. "Good stride these days," she notes with satisfaction. "She's not shuffling anymore."

It's a thrilling car ride for Jaytee this morning. We see both a cement truck and a dump truck. When we take him into the Head Start classroom, he gives Beth, his sister, and me a big good-bye hug. Once Shontel is delivered to school, it's back home.

Now I have a chance to ask Beth about Shontel and Jaytee's relative who gave them the Christmas gift cards. Beth shares the miraculous news: A distant aunt from the South had, through family channels, learned about the two, and is interested in adopting them. Furthermore, she has been a foster mom specializing in behaviorally disabled children for years! She has one adopted child.

"Now, she can't adopt them yet because the case with that Midwest placement debacle of last spring is not yet closed!" Beth explains, and adds, "But the aunt has been in regular contact with me and with the case worker. Earlier in the winter she even came for a visit. The kids are not aware of a possible adoption by her, but it's just plain good news for them right now that they have an aunt who cares about and remembers them at Christmas."

At ten o'clock, we deliver David to the church so he can clean. On the drive home I learn how his disabilities came about. As a premature infant, a slight rise in David's blood pressure due to too much stimulation – perhaps light, noise, or touch – caused tiny capillaries in his brain to burst, resulting in a brain bleed. A quarter century ago, it was not recognized how absolutely important it is to keep stimulation of any kind to a minimum with premature babies. When I ask a pediatrician friend about this later, she explains that those capillaries are only needed as the brain is developing before birth. A full term baby would no longer have those fragile capillaries. If only David had been born twenty-five years later.

Back at the house, Beth works at the table with her notebook and phone. First she deals with Jeffrey. Tuesday's appointments for him are complicated this week: separate parent visitations and speech therapy with Jeffrey, the dad, and dad's girlfriend. It is decided that the supervised visits will take place in the lounge of the hospital where speech therapy will happen, rather than the case worker's office. I ask Beth if she thinks his speech is just delayed or if he may never speak very much.

"I'm not sure; he sometimes says 'up' and points, usually down although he means up. He sometimes says 'Mama.' Mostly he doesn't speak or sign." This despite Beth's continual signing and prompting for language. Nevertheless, he's bright eyed and curious, and busy all the time. At this moment, he's imitating the teenagers in the house by carrying around a string pretending it's a set of ear buds.

Getting his transportation and supervision details set up today is important. The visitation days have been changed because of dad's work schedule, and she wants to make sure everyone's on the same page. Plus she has scheduled a personal appointment with her financial planner during that window of time, and those windows are rare.

Next are several phone calls related to the adult foster license she needs. One of the classes she needs to take is on Saturday morning while Shontel and Jaytee have swim lessons. "This is when I need a husband!" she bemoans. Fingerprinting for Coleen and David happen on Wednesdays. That's do-able.

Soon it is late morning and time to collect David and take Mercedes to dialysis. Beth checks with Coleen about Jeffrey who will need lunch and a nap. At three o'clock, Coleen and Jeffrey will need to walk over and pick up Shontel from school.

In the car, Beth tells me that having Coleen walk over pick up Shontel assures that she will get some fresh air and exercise every day. Aside from sorting and delivering the clean laundry, and taking care of Jeffrey for a few hours each day, she mostly watches TV or texts. Coleen's stamina is limited; I am thinking she could not work full time. While her routine might drive someone else crazy, she doesn't seem unhappy or bored.

When we arrive at the school, Mercedes is waiting on the front steps. "Finals tomorrow," she says. When we drop her off at the hospital, I'm pleasantly surprised that we don't pull into the parking lot but drive right up to the door. The girl is confident enough and physically strong enough to hop out, walk into the hospital, and sign in by herself.

On the way to a restaurant for lunch, we pass near some railroad tracks with several parked train cars. "I know that when

Jaytee's gone, I'll think of him whenever I'm driving and see a train or a crane or bulldozer." Beth says. During lunch she probably also is reminded of him because I knock my half-full glass over, and Beth, the waiter, and I mop up the table with a dozen napkins.

I mention that I need to buy some new walking shoes, and she suggests that when we're done with lunch, even though her day is already full, that we go find the store that carries the brand I want. I protest that she needn't do that, but she points out that this is an *adult* activity, rare in her day-to-day life. So before picking up Mercedes, we go shoe shopping.

At the dialysis center, we find a more subdued Mercedes. She has a headache and leans on Beth's arm while she talks with the nurses. A man with a young boy joins us in the elevator down to the lobby. The father announces to all, "He hasn't had a nap today so I'm not responsible for his behavior in this elevator." A woman comments that she has a young child and understands. Beth, Mercedes, and I say nothing; I suspect we're all thinking about the fact that Jaytee hasn't taken a nap in three years; at Head Start an aide does a quiet activity with him while the other children sleep. This boy just stands politely next to his father.

Headed back to the house, we stop to pick up Jaytee. Mercedes gets him while Beth and I wait in the car. When they come out, the girl is carrying a shopping bag of donated books for Jaytee to take home. It seems that each child has received a bagful.

After parking the van in the driveway, Beth chats for a few minutes on the sidewalk with the artist who lives across the street. She reports on the health of another neighbor, an elderly man who has taken ill this week, and whose son won't arrive until tomorrow. She and Beth discuss the decision by one family on the block to have their son apply to a private high school.

"You know, if he doesn't get in they might move." The artist says, shaking her head in disapproval.

"Bad idea," Beth says in agreement. You can't find another neighborhood like this one."

⤳◦

WHEN SHONTEL ARRIVES from school, she gets herself a bowl of chips and sits down immediately at the table next to Beth to do her homework. It's a two-sided sheet of math problems about place value, money, counting by tens, word addition problems, and time. Although the girl is willing to sit at the table, her attention constantly wonders.

Beth points to a sentence and reads a word problem that involves adding six and four and then an additional eight pieces of fruit. Shontel thoughtlessly offers some random numbers as possible answers, and then says, totally off topic, "I like to go to rivers in the cold weather."

"Why?" asks Beth. "You can't swim then."

"But I could skip rocks."

"Okay." says Beth, "What if you skip six rocks, and then I give you four more to skip, and then you skip eight more?"

"That's eighteen rocks." she immediately answers.

The small photocopied pictures of coins on her worksheet are tough to identify. Beth pulls a handful of change out of her purse, and they work the money problems with real coins. Likewise, the tiny analog clock faces on the page are difficult to make out. Beth takes a plate-sized paper clock with moveable hands out of her notebook. Even with the manipulative clock, telling time is hard for Shontel. However, she does move the clock hand around the dial to help her solve another addition problem. Because Beth needs to start dinner, she asks Shontel to complete the back of the worksheet by herself. However, without Beth's support, the girl stops thinking mathematically and simply fills in the blanks on the page with random numbers.

Beth tells me that she has talked with Shontel's teacher about the homework. The teacher says that it's to check for understanding. Beth comments that if a child doesn't understand it, she can't do it, and if she does understand it, she doesn't need the practice. If she completes the homework with help, it's not an accurate gauge of her understanding. I'm thinking that if Shontel has learned to just fill in the blanks with any old numbers, knowing that the homework is not closely checked, then she's learning a bad coping skill. Shontel has been getting help with math by being pulled out of the class with a small group. Starting this month, however, the special education teacher will instead come into her classroom to work with her and several others.

"If you want, email me occasionally and ask me how Shontel is doing." the special education teacher said.

"No," Beth asserted, "you email me once a month and tell me how she's doing." The teacher agreed to do so.

Jaytee is interested in his new books, especially an Eric Carle book about rubber ducks. He counts the ten ducks with me and mostly follows along as I read him the story, even occasionally restating what I have just read. Compared to last spring and summer, this is amazing behavior. Compared to other five year olds? That's another thing.

Shontel wants to read an issue of *Ladybug* magazine with me that she has found in the bag of books. We're almost through the magazine when it's time for dinner. She sets the table as she's expected to, but she takes a minimalist approach! There are the right number of plates, forks, paper towels, and glasses on the table, but it looks like a hurricane swept through the dining room. I quietly nudge the plates and forks around so that they're in front of places where people will sit.

We are having cheese and spinach ravioli tonight, plus we are making our own salads at the table. No two salads are alike. The choices include greens, blueberries, feta cheese, bacon bits, pine nuts, cucumbers, walnuts, and various salad dressings. Jaytee just has blueberries. Shontel wants only bacon and pine nuts, but she is persuaded to have some greens.

Markie brings up her evening guitar lesson. She hasn't practiced at all this week, and Mercedes asks her why.

"I didn't have time," she responds. With mild disgust, Mercedes names all the times during the last few days when she could have practiced. Time management is definitely not one of Markie's strengths.

Jeffrey doesn't throw up tonight, and Jaytee doesn't spill his milk. I suppose I gave Beth her quota of spilled beverages for the day at lunch. Shontel's mood continues to deteriorate throughout dinner, and by the end of the meal she is playing with her food to get attention and making snide comments under her breath in response to anything said. Her face has a pinched look, so different from this morning. She doesn't seem tired, but maybe I just don't know her well enough to read her particular signs of fatigue.

Sure enough, not long after dinner she's in trouble for one too many smart aleck remarks. Beth tried to head this off by taking Shontel onto her lap and talking and laughing with her, but the girl seemed determined to get herself in hot water. Eventually, hot water is the actual solution, as Coleen supervises a bath.

When the dinner dishes are taken care, Beth and I drop Markie off for her guitar lesson at the community center and return home to get Jeffrey ready for bed. She and Coleen share the supervision of Jaytee's bath, and then all three young ones are in bed before we go back to pick up Markie.

On the way home, Markie is enthused about her lesson. "I learned two chords: E minor and one other one. I can't remember what it's called."

"E major?" I offer.

"Yes! That's it!"

After Markie has gone to her room, Beth explains that she doesn't really know if Markie will be able to learn to play the guitar, but she loves her lessons. Mercedes will be starting piano lessons later in the week, and is excited to do so. She probably missed band and chorus opportunities because of her health issues, so this might be her first exposure to making music since elementary school, assuming her school even had music classes. There's no piano in Beth's house. She'll have to practice on an electric keyboard.

David comes half way across the living, gets down on one knee, and gives me a short speech that makes little sense to me. Beth explains that it's the passage from his book where the man is proposing to his vacuum cleaner. I guess I've just had a marriage proposal of sorts!

"David, you're being silly. Marriage proposals are irritating and inappropriate for company. I think it's time for you to go take a shower and shave." He accepts her suggestion without being offended and cheerfully heads downstairs.

Midway through a conversation about what books we've been reading, Beth and I are suddenly interrupted by Markie. "Mama, Mama! Guess what! You know the little plants from the greenhouse in my room that weren't doing so good? Five out of four of them are going to live!"

"Mmm..." Beth says. I can tell, is considering whether or not to discuss mathematical thinking. "I don't think they'll live if they don't get some light. Your room is pretty dark."

"I'll give them light when they're older," she says, leaving the room.

"Well, okay then," Beth chuckles quietly.

We resume our conversation, and she's patient with my questions.

"What about your bedroom? It isn't locked. I've been wondering all year why kids don't go in there. After all, it's the place where you keep confiscated toys, presents, and off-limits foods for specific kids."

"Well, any transgression gets dealt with swiftly." she says firmly. I believe it. Even as a guest, I can feel the taboo against entering her room. It is part of the culture of the house, necessary for her sanity, I'm sure.

I also ask her about Jeffrey's dad. If he completes the last two sessions of his class, required because of his past abusive behavior, then the child will start to have longer visits and unsupervised visits with him. Eventually, visits will lengthen to several days at a time. If Jeffrey doesn't lose weight during those visits, they will gradually increase with the goal of the father taking custody. It won't happen overnight, Beth explains.

I bring up Mercedes demonstrations of affection for the little ones. Beth tells me how the girl is beginning, with the help of counseling, to let go of her hopes for reuniting with her father or the ex-girlfriend. The woman told the case worker last fall that she wanted to be Mercedes's foster mom. The caseworker explained she needed to visit on a regular basis, but she has not contacted the girl, nor visited once.

I ask her if it's going to drive her crazy to continue to care for Markie as she enters adulthood, since Markie's nonstop chatter is a challenge for most everyone, including Beth. She answers that she's used to her. I'm thinking that her decision is a no-nonsense blend of compassion and economic reality, although she doesn't tell me that. This living situation will benefit both Markie and Beth, since the young woman will continue to stay with the only family she's ever known and keep her dog, and Beth will continue to receive a monthly allowance for her care. Maybe it's more than that, though. Maybe I'm discounting how love works. Maybe there's a deeper and more affectionate relationship between the two than what I've been able to observe in my visits.

It suddenly dawns on me that this is her time, not kid time, and she doesn't need to be talking about kid issues. So I stop asking questions. We continue to talk, though, about books, basketball, and religion. We talk too long; all of a sudden it's midnight, and we head for bed. If I had known that Jaytee would wake her up at four-thirty the next morning, I would have been more responsible about the time.

A January Tuesday

Beth has been up for a long time when I rise at seven. It seems that Jaytee woke up at four-thirty, and woke up his sister. Although she shushed them and told them to go back to sleep, she's doubtful that they really did, and they were both out of bed at six-thirty. It might be a long day for everyone.

Shontel wants to make a lunch rather than have the free lunch provided at school. She makes herself a hotdog bun, cheese, and mustard sandwich. Beth gives her a juice box and a granola bar from her bedroom supplies to take with her.

Mercedes needs to be delivered to school a little earlier today because of finals, which means Jaytee also gets to the Head Start classroom a little early. He's the first one there, and the teacher's aide greets him warmly.

Back home, Beth works on Shontel's hair while she talks on the phone with the case worker. Jeffrey's dad is sick, and won't be able to visit today. Mom's appearance is always in doubt. The speech therapy appointment following the supervised visits is for dad and mom as much as for Jeffrey so that they can learn how to encourage language. Beth doesn't need that training. If neither biological parent is there, nor the dad's girlfriend, the appointment will be cancelled. Both the dad's illness and the possibility of no speech appointment change Jeffrey's pick-up time and perhaps the drop-off time. It's decided that the case worker will page Beth, who will be at her financial advisor's office, if she needs to reconnect with Jeffrey earlier than planned. I tell her that I imagine these last minute changes are common.

"If the parents were dependable and responsible, their kids wouldn't be in foster care," she notes.

A glance at the clock and she realizes that it's almost time for Shontel's school to start. Beth grabs her car keys, and we head out the door.

"I could have walked her to school," I say. "I didn't think of it. Why didn't you ask?"

"It's okay," she says. And it turns out it is, because the conversation in the van is important.

"I'll be picking you up early today because you have an appointment with Anita." Beth tells Shontel.

"Anita helps me with my handwriting, right, Mom?"

"No, it's playing with toys in Connie's office that will help you with your handwriting."

"Why do I see Anita?" Shontel asks, though in the past she has been able to state exactly why she sees her.

"So you can talk about your feelings," Beth answers.

"Mom, I want to stay with you until I'm really old, like twenty-eight."

Calmly and tenderly, Beth answers as we turn the corner. "That won't work. I'll be too old then."

"Yes it will. You're old now and you're not dead yet."

With that said, we arrive at the school, and Shontel hops out just as the five-minute bell is chiming.

Back at the dining room table, Beth reads the morning's mail. There's a court summons to testify regarding Jeffrey's birth mom, probably a hearing to decide whether she's fit to parent his little sister. There is a flyer about an upcoming class for care givers of children whose academic learning disabilities make school challenging. She's interested, but there aren't enough hours in the week. She muses that it's always interesting to get a child with an issue that's new to her. As an example, she explains that when she cared for a girl with anorexia, she learned all about the disorder.

It's now almost time for the driver to pick Jeffrey up for his appointment. He is spiffily dressed, his hair is combed, and his diaper bag is packed. Coleen is upstairs ready to watch him for a few minutes until he's picked up. I sit on the couch with her and ask about her sister's child.

"She's four, and really tall, like my twin brother," Coleen tells me in a combination of words and sign.

"Your brother is not your twin brother. He's just a brother. He's a year older than you," Beth explains.

It's heartbreaking to see how underdeveloped Coleen's language skills are, despite specialized schooling until she was twenty-one. She does not live in a community of signers, so her fluency is limited, nor does she participate in much of the oral conversation going on around her. Most of the language she gets comes from captions on the television or texts on her phone. It's a dilemma not just for Coleen but for many with her extreme hearing loss. I am also beginning to realize that her fragile physical health puts her in a tough spot. Like Jeffrey, she has huge nutritional challenges. Her willowy body is not that way by choice and she struggles to maintain an adequate weight. Food allergies and delicate lungs add to the mix.

"Your sister lives with her boyfriend?" I ask.

"No, he cheated on her, so she dumped him."

"Do you see her much?"

"Sometimes. Not too much," she responds. I'm thinking that if her sister doesn't sign, it limits their ability to interact on a deep level. Hopefully, they text each other frequently.

Soon it's time for me to go home. I have a commitment this afternoon, one place I have to be, and it's time for Beth to leave for her appointment, which she miraculously squeezed into the morning, just one of the many places she has to be today. As I head for the car, I take out my new keychain, the one tangible thing I am carrying away from Sylvia Street. My head is full though. It's a new year and new possibilities abound.

Jeffrey might get to live with his father. Shontel and Jaytee have an aunt who may adopt them. Mercedes may learn to play the piano and get healthy enough for a kidney transplant. Maybe Coleen's relationship with her sister will continue to grow thanks to the gift of texting. Markie may even learn to the play the guitar. In the meantime, the house on Sylvia Street hums along with affection and humor.

My Writing Desk

ABOVE THE DESK where I write is a twelve-by-twenty-four-inch colorful photo and paper collage of my family that my artistic daughter created for me. It makes us look like a large family, even though there's only me, my two children, their spouses, and my three grandchildren. This is because there are multiple pictures of each of us, including baby and childhood photos of the adults. Only the two black and white pictures of me at ages one and three, and maybe a Dukes of Hazzard T-shirt on my son-in-law at about age seven suggest that over sixty years of time are represented.

I'm thinking that if Beth had a similar collage, with only one picture for each child, the collage would have to run along the entire lengths of both the west and the south walls of the room to include everyone.

I play with some numbers: A child needs about five thousand diapers over three years. Having only one child in diapers at a time for thirty years would mean changing almost fifty thousand diapers. Having four school-aged children in the house at one time with three report cards a year for thirty years would mean reading three hundred and sixty report cards. Or take socks: say there are five kids in the house, using seven pairs a week each; thirty-five pairs a week times fifty-six weeks a year times thirty years means washing fifty-eight thousand pairs of socks.

Those are the easy numbers. Harder to calculate are things like how many hugs? How many fevers? How many dressings changed, or IV's administered? How many math problems at the dining table?

How do you see life? You win if you die with the most toys? It's a dog-eat-dog world? According to Audrey Hepburn, the most important thing is to be happy. Mark Twain said you need good books, good friends, and a sleepy conscience. The house on Sylvia Street has me thinking about this.

It's late February, and the daily emailed quotes my friend sends in late winter in her series she calls "Pathways to Peace" have been arriving each day. I reread yesterday's message with Beth's life, as I've watched it over the last year, in mind. It said:

Fundamentally, helping, fixing and serving are ways of seeing life. When you help, you see life as weak. When you fix, you see life as broken. When you serve, however, you see life as whole.

After a year of observation, I'm ready to say unequivocally that Beth lives with a sense of wholeness that is rare in our world.

BIBLIOGRAPHY

Blackshere, Ryan. 50% of Foster Care Kids Don't Graduate High School". *NBC News, Education Nation.* Accessed May 25, 2012. http://www.educationnation.com.

BrainyQuote. "Life quotes". Accessed February 25, 2013. http://www.brainyquote.com/quotes/topics/topic_life.html.

Bureau of Indian Education. "Schools." Accessed February 25, 2013. http://bie.edu/Schools/index/htm

"Deadline Nears to Report Jesuit Abuse". *Yakima Herald Republic.* October 3, 2009. http://www.bishop-accountability.org.

Friends of the Astoria Column, Inc. "The Astoria Column: Where History Takes Off." Accessed February 19, 2013. http://www.astoriacolumn.org.

Gage, Bruce. "The Growing Problems of Cognitive Disorders in Corrections". *Iceberg.* Vol. 19, no 2 (June 2009). Accessed May 25th, 2012. http://www.faciceberg.org/newsletters.

Hmong American Partnership. "2010 Census Hmong Population by State". Accessed May 25, 2012. http://www.hmong.org .

"Interesting Statistics on Family Dinners". Accessed March 24, 2012. http://dinnertrade.com/568/interesting-statistics-on-family-dinners.

Lawrence Livermore National Laboratory. "Marshal Islands Dose Assessment and RadioecologyProgram." Accessed August 7, 2012 . https://marshallislands.llnl.gov/newsletter.php.

Lupus Foundation of America. "What is Lupus?" Accessed March 20, 2012. http://www.lupus.org/webmodules/webarticlesnet/templates/new.

National Indian Child Welfare Association. "ICWA/Child Protective Services (CPS) Flow Chart." Accessed March 23, 2012. http://nicwa.org/.

Ostrom, Carol. "Kidney Failure: a case study in consequences of entitlement." *The Seattle Times*. January 20, 2013.

Radic, Theo. "Nuclear Testing in the Pacific Ocean and Nevada." Accessed August 7, 2012. www.angelfire.com/sk/syukhtun/pacificbombs.html.

Sullivan, Jennifer. "Tribe Takes Control of Child Welfare from State." Seattle Times. March 29, 2012.

Taylor, Alan. "When We Tested Nuclear Bombs." In Focus. *The Atlantic*. May 6, 2011. http://www.theatlantic.com/infocus/2011/05/when-we-tested-nuclear-bombs/100061/.

Wikipedia. "Pacific Proving Grounds." Accessed August 7, 2012. http://en.wikipedia.org/wiki/Pacific_Proving_Grounds.

Book Club Discussion Starters

1. The narrative spans from March to January. Which change over time in one of the children do you find most interesting?

2. Throughout the year, the author grows in her understanding of the life stories of the children. Some of what she finds out is surprising. Which life story surprised you the most?

3. The author has written about someone else, but she interjects herself into the narrative. Imagine yourself shadowing this family throughout the year. How might you be changed?

4. There are two types of chapters in the book: those based on time – days of the week, and those based on place – principally rooms in the house. The author has referred to these as "two different types of beads on a narrative string." How effective is this structure?

5. The phrases "purpose-driven life" and "inner compass" are used to describe Beth. Do you agree with the author's use of these phrases? Why or why not?

6. Talking about foster care means talking about society and social issues. Which issue addressed in the book seems most compelling to you?

ABOUT THE AUTHOR

JUDY BORDEAUX LIVES in the Cascade foothills east of Seattle. In addition to writing, she currently works part time as a curriculum developer after spending thirty-seven years as an English teacher and elementary school librarian. She facilitates workshops, performs as a storyteller, and sings lower first alto in the Seattle Women's Chorus. Mostly, though, she delights in being the grandmother to three wonderful girls.

Made in the USA
Charleston, SC
05 April 2014